The Notes:
A Visual Companion for Students

to accompany

Psychology

Sixth Edition

John W. Santrock

University of Texas, Dallas

Boston   Burr Ridge, IL   Dubuque, IA   Madison, WI   New York   San Francisco   St. Louis
Bangkok   Bogotá   Caracas   Lisbon   London   Madrid
Mexico City   Milan   New Delhi   Seoul   Singapore   Sydney   Taipei   Toronto

McGraw-Hill Higher Education

A Division of The **McGraw-Hill** *Companies*

The Notes: A Visual Companion for Students to accompany
PSYCHOLOGY, SIXTH EDITION

This book is printed on acid-free paper.

2 3 4 5 6 7 8 9 0 CUS/CUS 9 0 3 2 1 0

ISBN 0-07-237191-9

www.mhhe.com

Table of Contents

INTRODUCTION

Welcome to the first edition of *The Notes: A Visual Companion for Students* to accompany *Psychology*, 6/e by John Santrock.

How often do you find yourself asking these questions:

What exactly is this graph telling me?

Why is the information in this chart important?

What is this diagram supposed to teach me?

A picture can tell a thousand words—so states the old truthful adage. Here, the perfect "little something extra" to complete your learning tools package—at last, a study tool that helps you make sense of the pictures! To know and understand your psychology textbook means more than just knowing and understanding what you *read*—it also means being able to interpret and comprehend what you *see*.

Containing images taken directly from the main text, this visual note companion serves to supplement the new and improved *Student Study Guide* that also accompanies *Psychology*, Sixth Edition.

TIPS on how to use *The Notes*:

1. The images are compiled and organized by chapter. Look carefully at each and ask yourself these four essential questions:

- Why does the author choose to illustrate this concept?

- What kind of information does the picture provide?

- Why is it important?

- How is it supposed to help me?

2. Write your answers and interpretations on the lines provided—feel free to mark up the graphs, charts, or diagrams any way you wish—use highlighters, colored pencils, even crayons—anything that will help you learn and understand the information the best way possible.

For Graphs:

- What data is being represented here?

- What relationship among the variables can I identify?

For Charts:

- What main points are being detailed?

- What does the information mean to me?

(Use the spaces provided to rewrite the terms, concepts, theories in your own words)

For Diagrams:

- What is going on in this picture? Why is this particular concept being illustrated?

- How does the picture support the text?

More Study Tips for the Successful Student

1.	TAKE NOTES: LISTEN before you write. Try to grasp the main ideas of your instructor's lecture, then rather than writing down *everything* you hear verbatim, try to organize your notes in outline form. For example, your instructor has decided to lecture on dreams. Your notes could look something like this:

I.	Dreams

A.	The Stages of sleep

    1.	stage 1 - transition

    2.	stage 2 - deeper sleep

    3.	stage 3 - slow brain waves

    4.	stage 4 - deepest sleep

B.	Four views

    1.	Unconscious wish fulfillment (Freud)

    2.	Reverse-learning theory

    3.	Dreams-for-survival theory

    4.	Activation-synthesis theory

C.	Symbols

    1.	Climbing a stairway — sexual intercourse

    2.	Bullets, fire, snakes — male sex organs

    3.	Ovens, boxes, tunnels — female sex organs

D.	Types

    1.	Daydreams

    2.	Nightmares

    3.	Lucid dreams

Note that there are no full sentences—try to listen for the main points, then jot them down quickly.

2.	REVIEW YOUR NOTES: The best time to review your notes is as soon as possible after a lecture. Don't wait until the next class to review your notes. Don't wait until the night before an exam to review them either and expect to absorb weeks' worth of information in one long night.

3.	THE SQ3R METHOD: This method has been tried and tested and students have had much success with it. The process includes:

Survey: Review the chapter outline for a quick overview. Peruse the material and take note of the major headings, charts, pictures.

Question: Ask yourself questions about the material. Refer to the learning objectives or chapter outline, which often details the major points. You may want to take some of the major headings and turn them into questions.

Read: After you've completed your list of questions, read through the chapter material, which will now appear more meaningful to you. Taking notes as you read will help you further grasp major concepts, theories, and points.

Recite: Read by section. Once you've completed each section, try to answer some of those questions you formulated earlier. Read out loud. Oftentimes recitation will help make the material even more comprehensive.

Review: After you've completed reading an entire chapter, review it. Go over the lists of questions and answers you've written for yourself; take note of anything that demands further clarification—points you'd like to ask your professor during class or during a student-instructor conference. Again, do not wait weeks or days after reading the material to review it. Return to it as soon as possible.

4.   ORGANIZE: Some of you hold down several part-time jobs and take on full course loads. Be careful not to burn yourself out. Be aware of how much time you have to work with—make sure to schedule enough hours in the week to study your materials, work, and rest! Gather all your materials into a manageable order: your text, class notes, old exams, study guides, and assess how much time you'll need to review everything. Then set aside a reasonable amount of time in your schedule to sit down quietly and study.

We hope you find *The Notes* to be an effective study tool. Good luck!

The Notes

Chapter 1 What is Psychology?

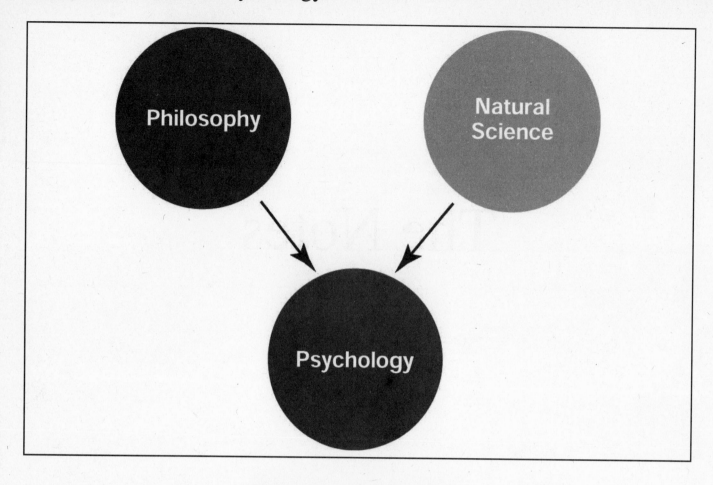

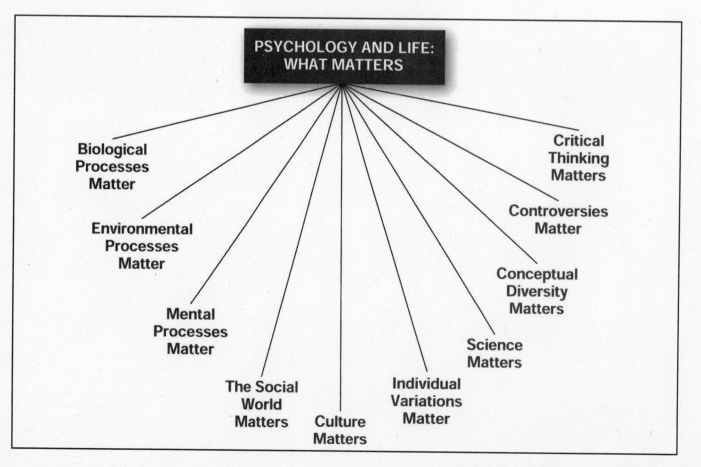

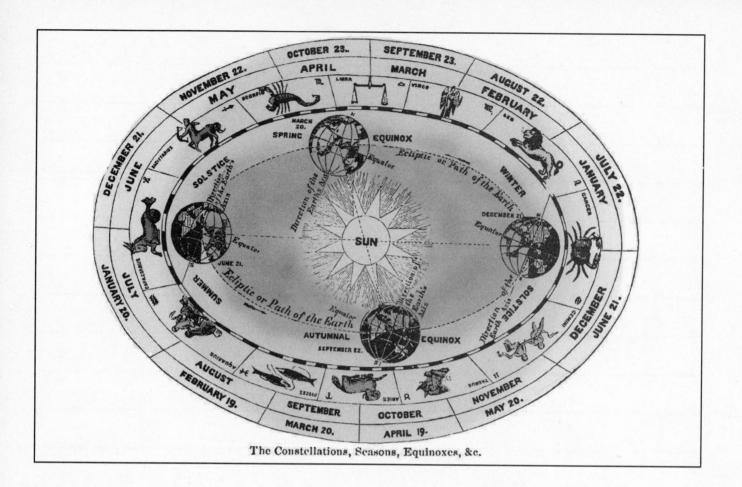

The Constellations, Seasons, Equinoxes, &c.

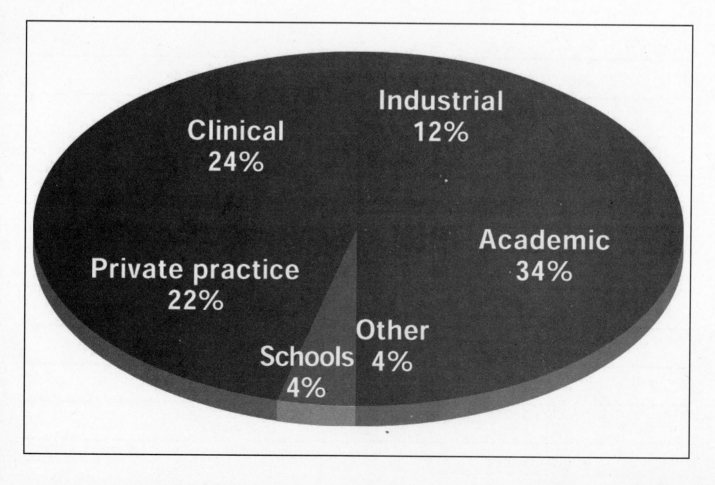

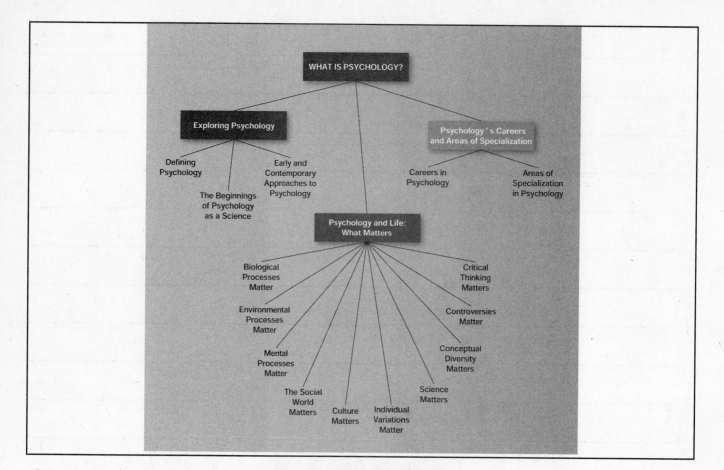

Chapter 2 Psychology's Scientific Methods

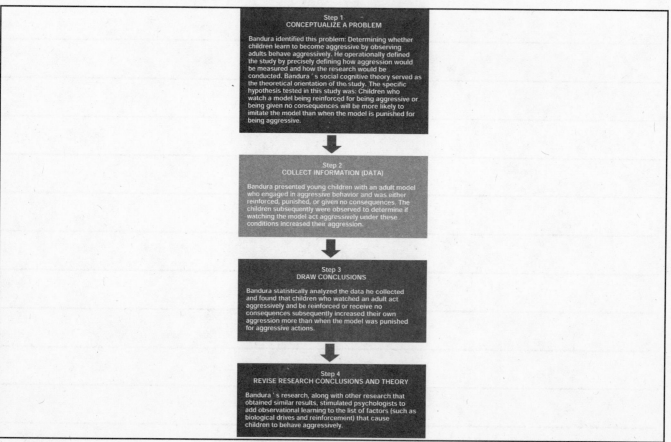

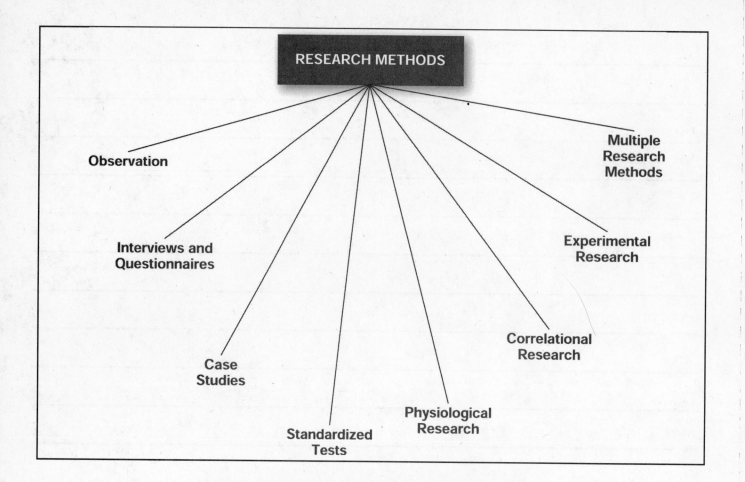

RESEARCH METHODS

Observation

Multiple Research Methods

Interviews and Questionnaires

Experimental Research

Case Studies

Correlational Research

Standardized Tests

Physiological Research

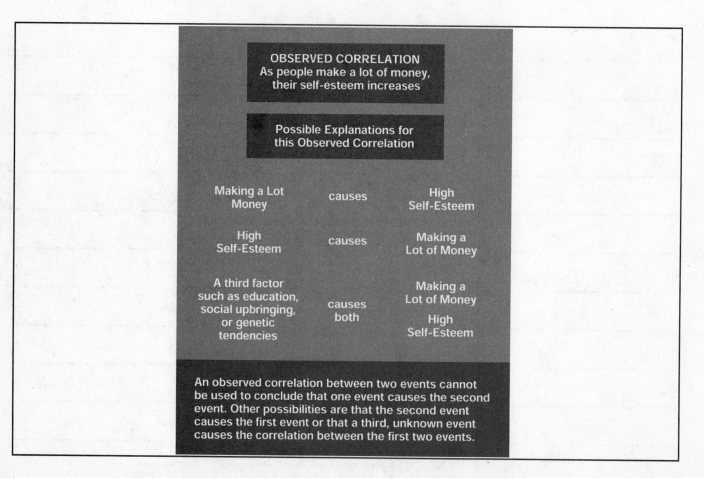

OBSERVED CORRELATION
As people make a lot of money, their self-esteem increases

Possible Explanations for this Observed Correlation

Making a Lot Money	causes	High Self-Esteem
High Self-Esteem	causes	Making a Lot of Money
A third factor such as education, social upbringing, or genetic tendencies	causes both	Making a Lot of Money / High Self-Esteem

An observed correlation between two events cannot be used to conclude that one event causes the second event. Other possibilities are that the second event causes the first event or that a third, unknown event causes the correlation between the first two events.

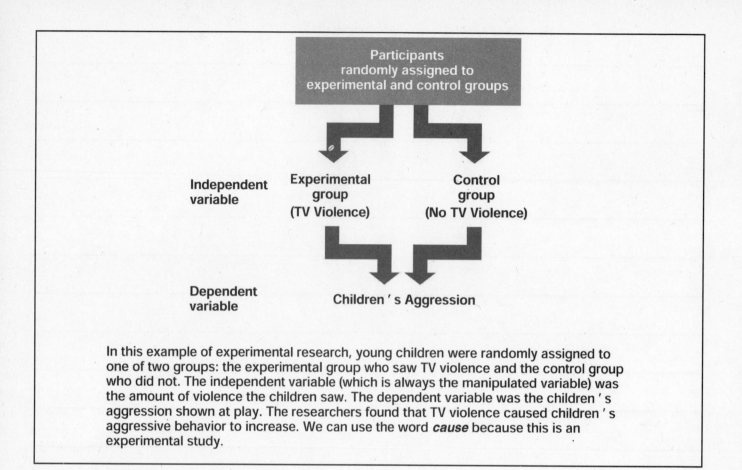

Participants randomly assigned to experimental and control groups

Independent variable

Experimental group (TV Violence)

Control group (No TV Violence)

Dependent variable

Children's Aggression

In this example of experimental research, young children were randomly assigned to one of two groups: the experimental group who saw TV violence and the control group who did not. The independent variable (which is always the manipulated variable) was the amount of violence the children saw. The dependent variable was the children's aggression shown at play. The researchers found that TV violence caused children's aggressive behavior to increase. We can use the word *cause* because this is an experimental study.

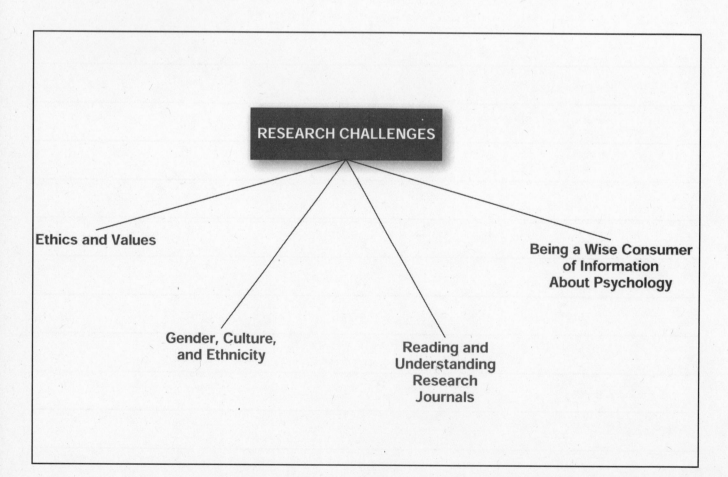

RESEARCH CHALLENGES

Ethics and Values

Being a Wise Consumer of Information About Psychology

Gender, Culture, and Ethnicity

Reading and Understanding Research Journals

Chapter 3 Biological Foundations and Neuroscience

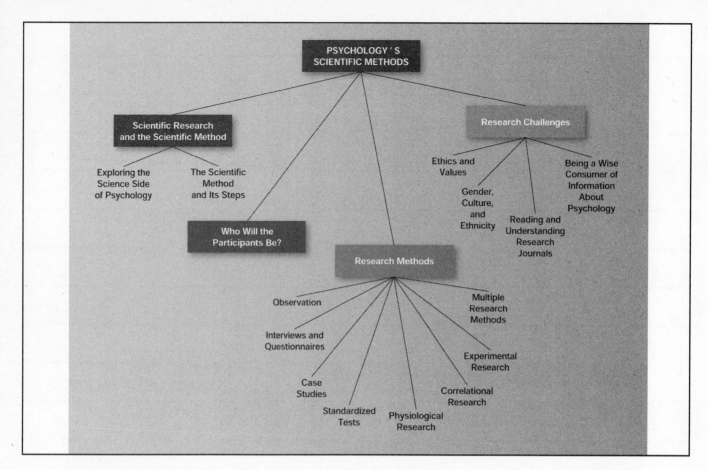

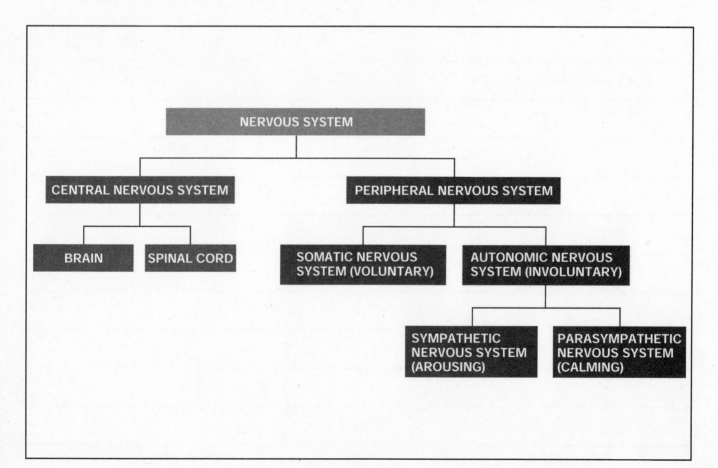

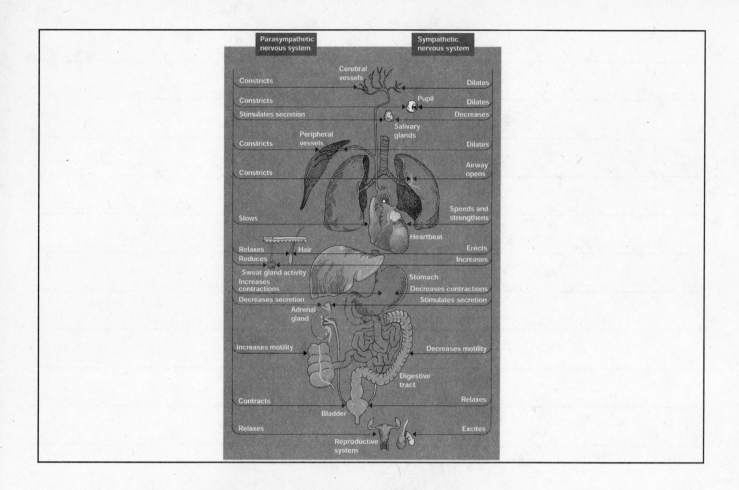

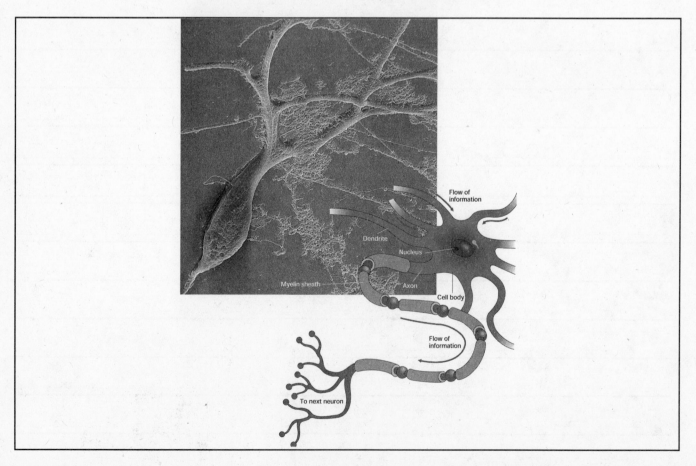

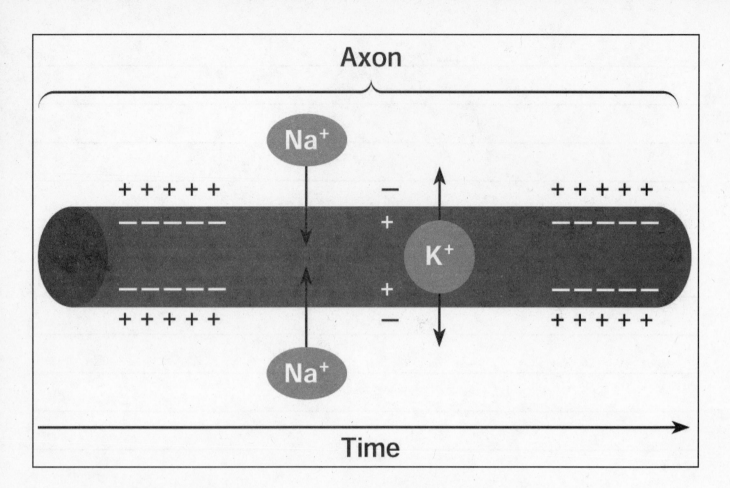

Axon

Na⁺

K⁺

Na⁺

Time

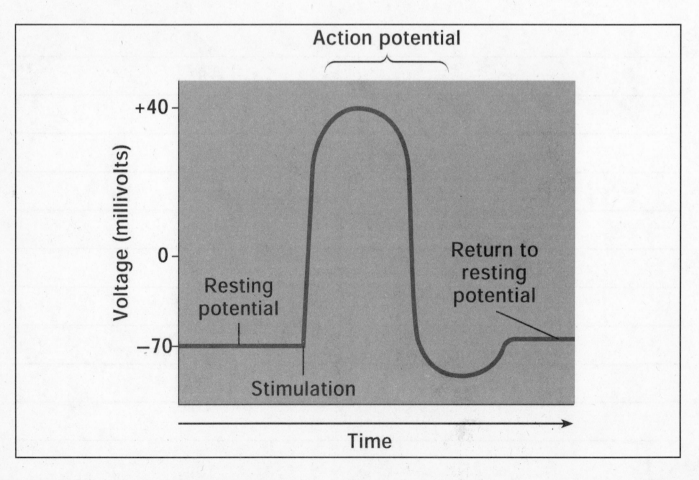

Action potential

+40

0

Voltage (millivolts)

−70

Resting potential

Stimulation

Return to resting potential

Time

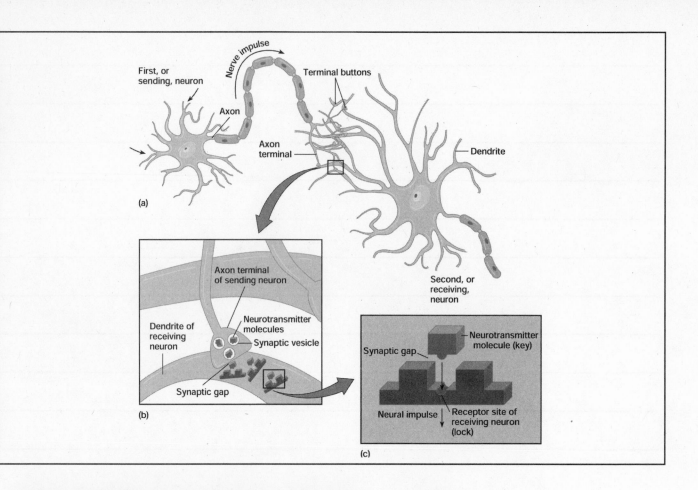

First, or sending, neuron

Nerve impulse

Axon

Terminal buttons

Axon terminal

Dendrite

(a)

Second, or receiving, neuron

Axon terminal of sending neuron

Neurotransmitter molecules

Dendrite of receiving neuron

Synaptic vesicle

Synaptic gap

(b)

Synaptic gap

Neurotransmitter molecule (key)

Neural impulse

Receptor site of receiving neuron (lock)

(c)

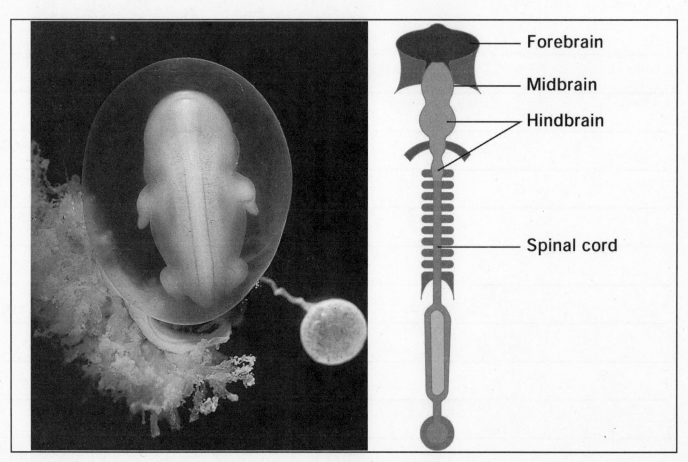

Forebrain

Midbrain

Hindbrain

Spinal cord

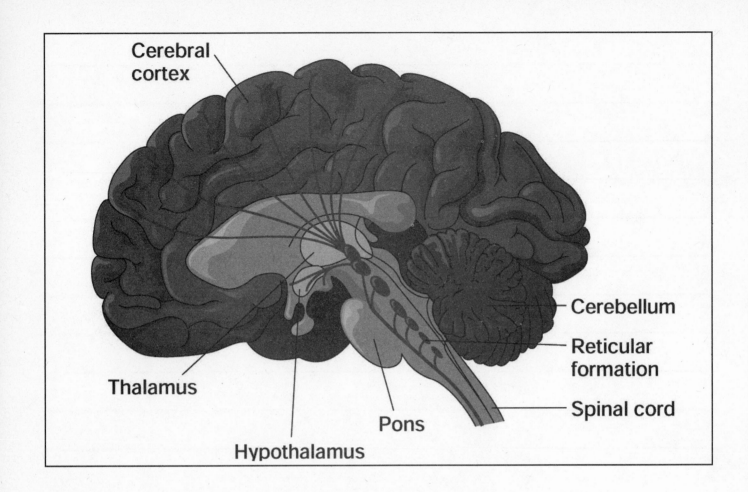

Cerebral cortex

Cerebellum

Reticular formation

Spinal cord

Thalamus

Pons

Hypothalamus

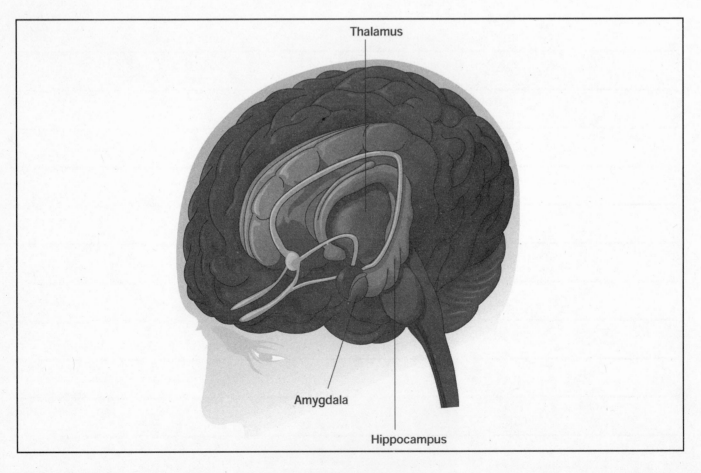

Thalamus

Amygdala

Hippocampus

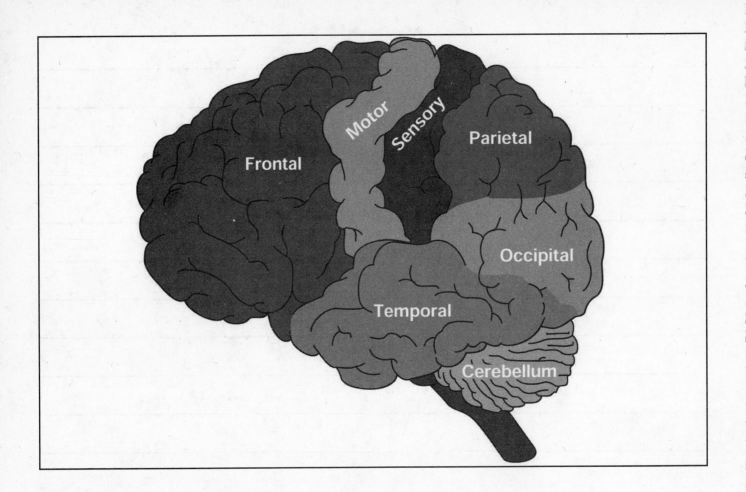

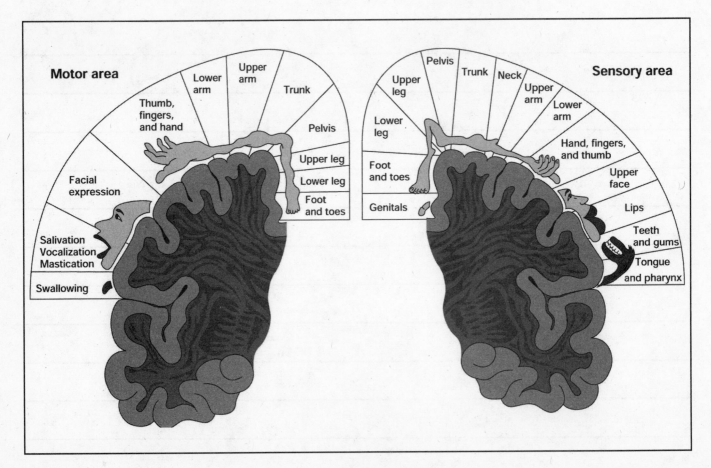

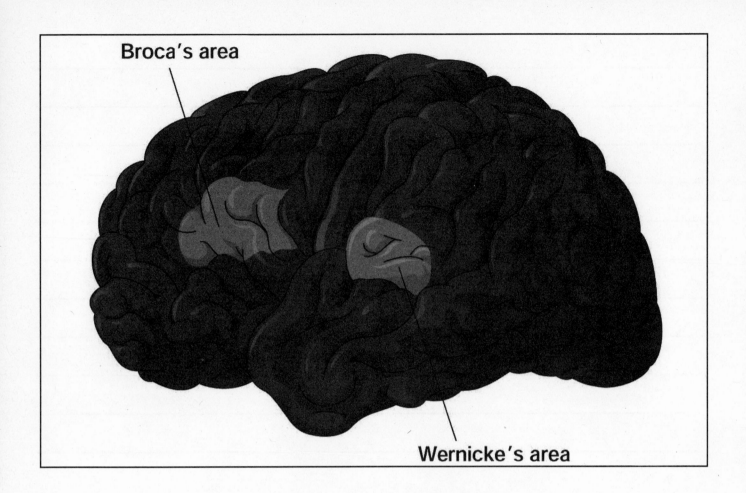

Broca's area

Wernicke's area

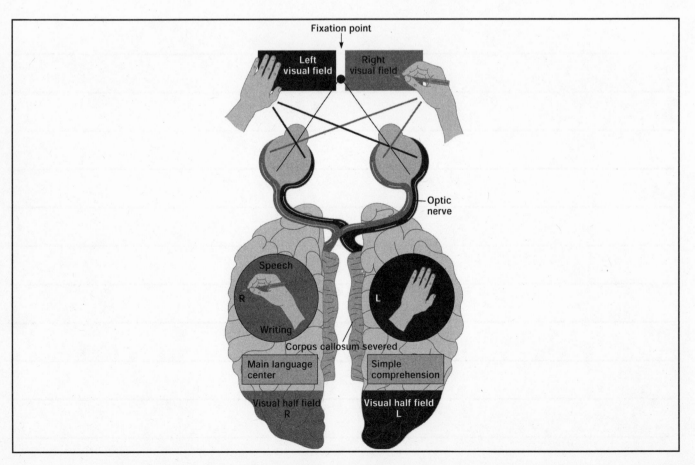

Fixation point

Left visual field

Right visual field

Optic nerve

Speech

R

L

Writing

Corpus callosum severed

Main language center

Simple comprehension

Visual half field R

Visual half field L

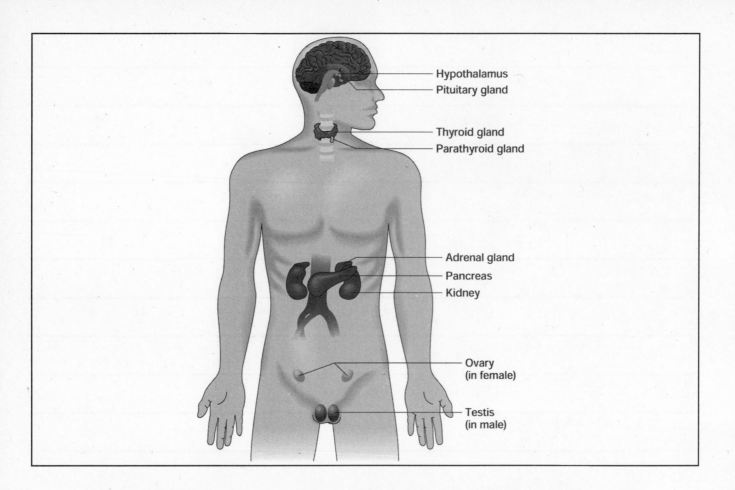

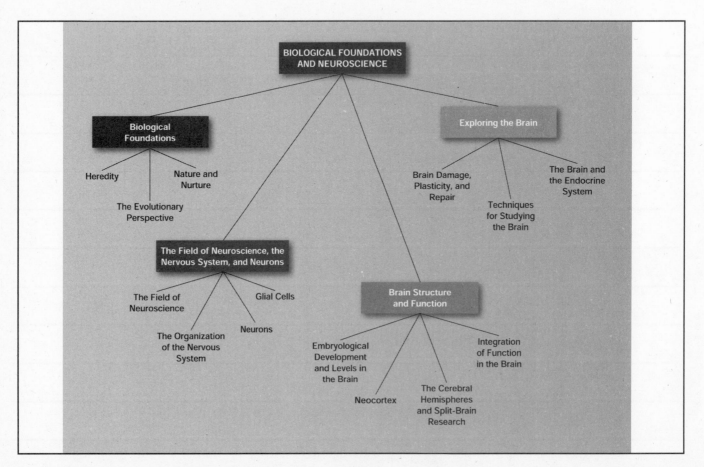

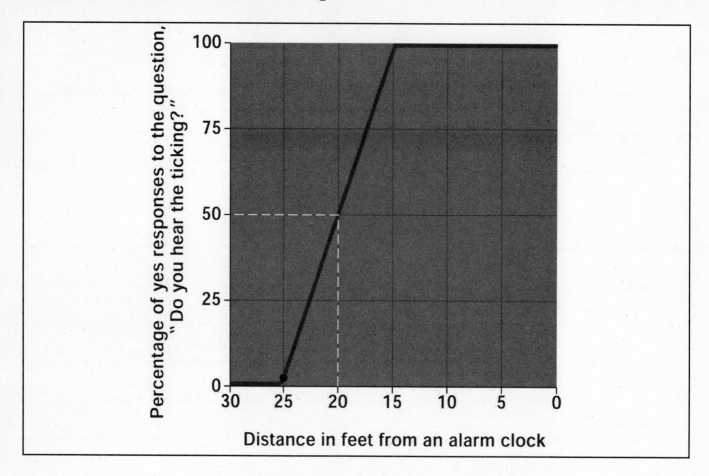

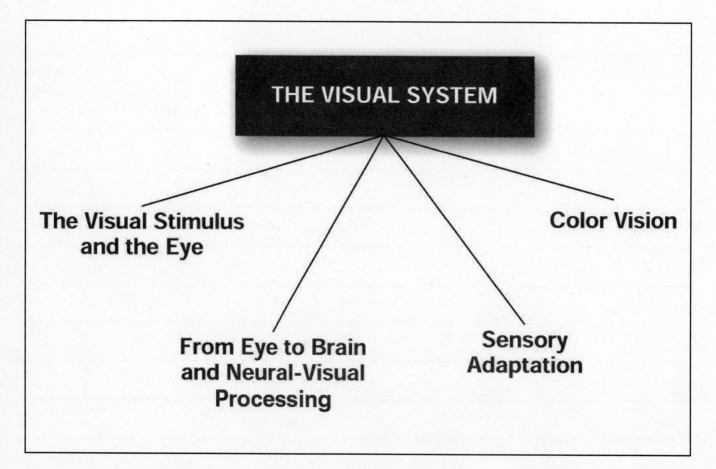

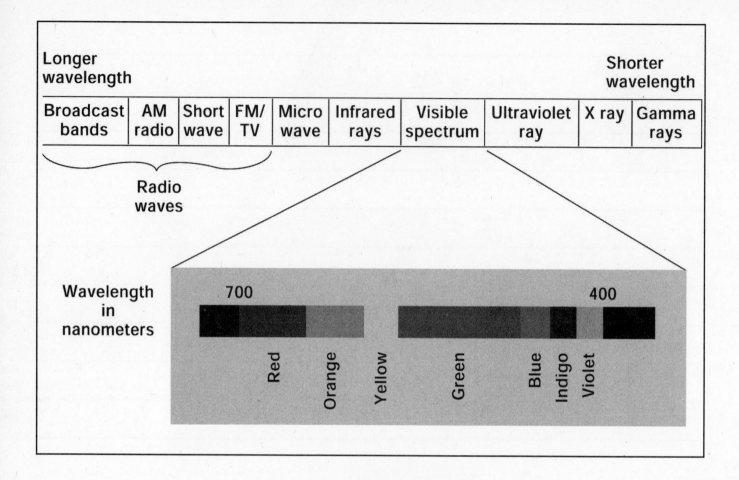

Longer
wavelength

Shorter
wavelength

Broadcast bands	AM radio	Short wave	FM/ TV	Micro wave	Infrared rays	Visible spectrum	Ultraviolet ray	X ray	Gamma rays

Radio
waves

Wavelength
in
nanometers

700

400

Red

Orange

Yellow

Green

Blue

Indigo

Violet

Retina

Sclera

Retinal blood vessels

Optic nerve

Blind spot

Fovea

Lens

Iris

Pupil

Cornea

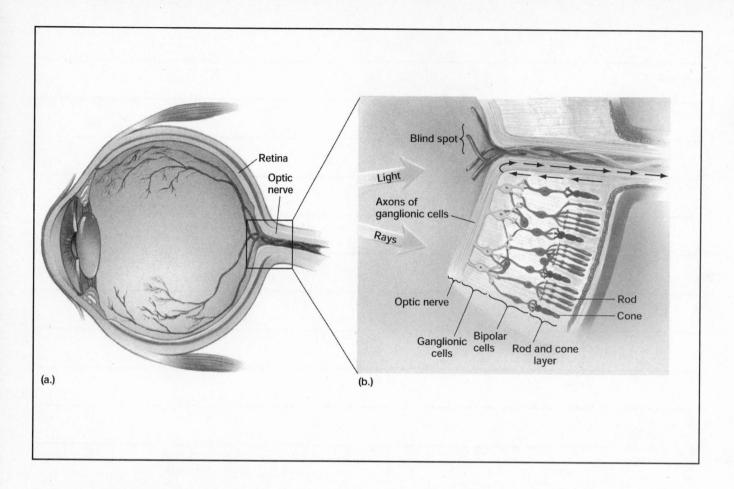

(a.)

Retina

Optic nerve

Blind spot

Light

Axons of ganglionic cells

Rays

Optic nerve

Ganglionic cells

Bipolar cells

Rod and cone layer

Rod

Cone

(b.)

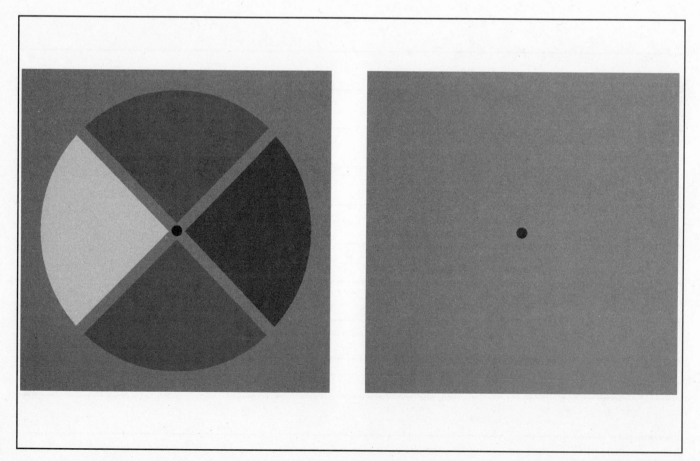

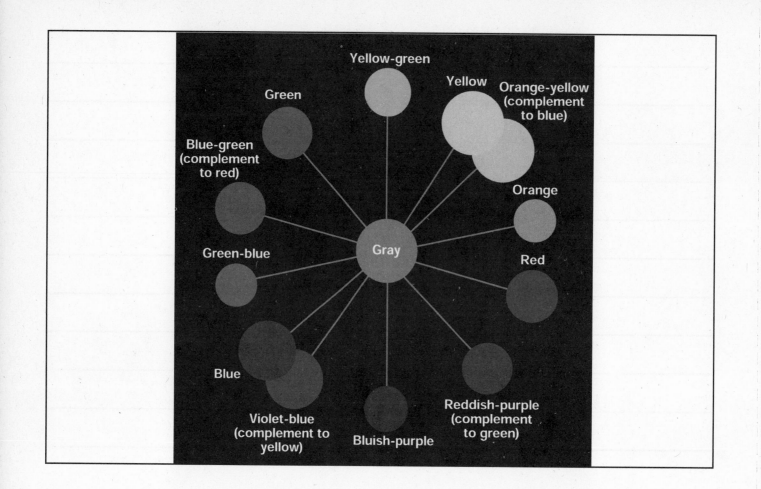

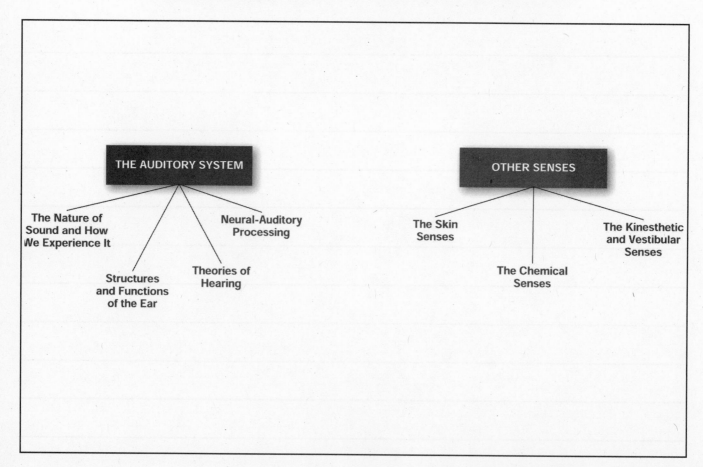

34

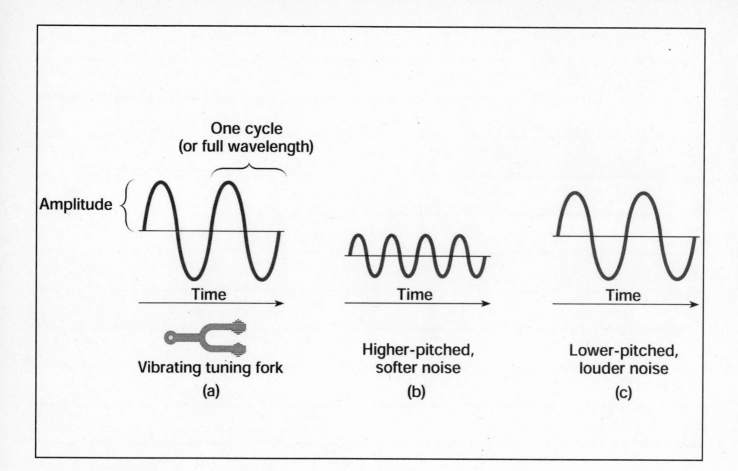

One cycle
(or full wavelength)

Amplitude

Time

Vibrating tuning fork

(a)

Time

Higher-pitched,
softer noise

(b)

Time

Lower-pitched,
louder noise

(c)

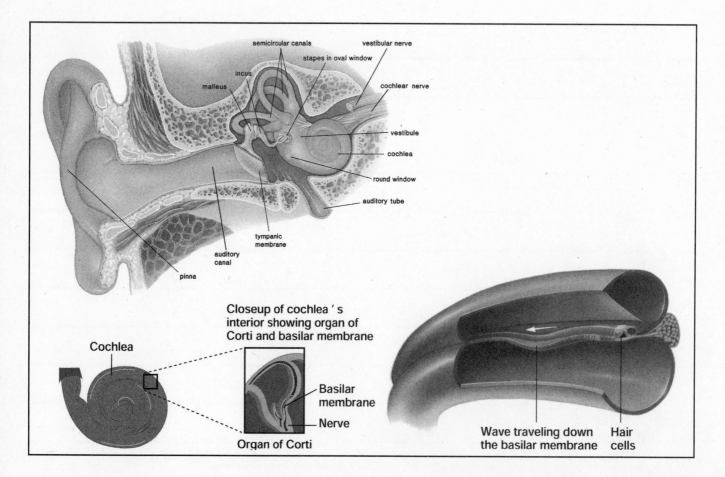

semicircular canals

vestibular nerve

stapes in oval window

malleus

incus

cochlear nerve

vestibule

cochlea

round window

auditory tube

tympanic
membrane

auditory
canal

pinna

Closeup of cochlea's
interior showing organ of
Corti and basilar membrane

Cochlea

Basilar
membrane

Nerve

Organ of Corti

Wave traveling down
the basilar membrane

Hair
cells

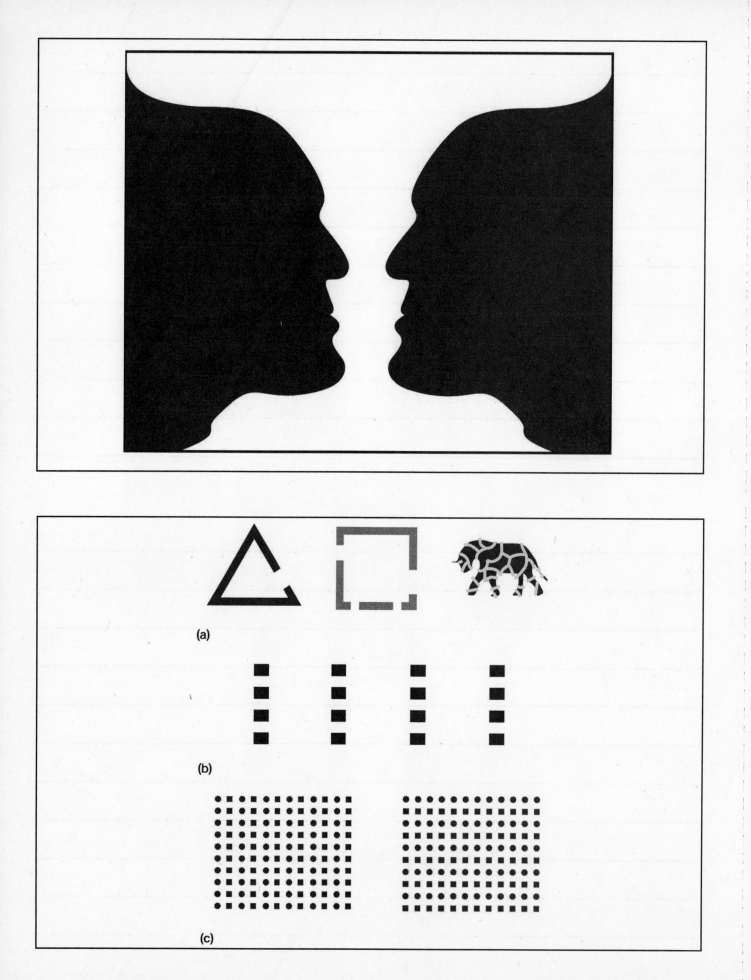

(a)

(b)

(c)

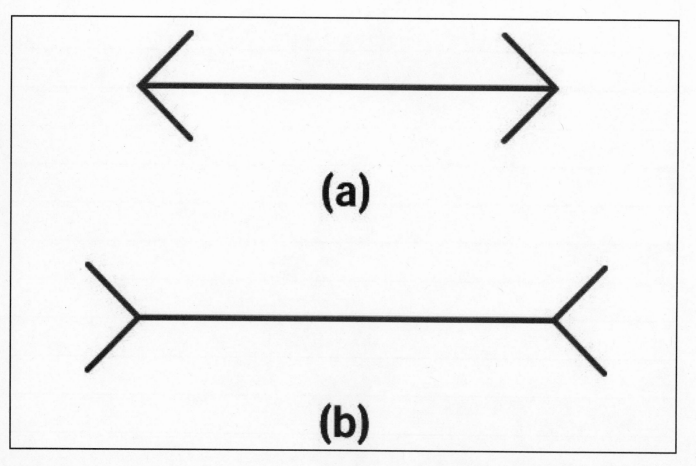

(a)

(b)

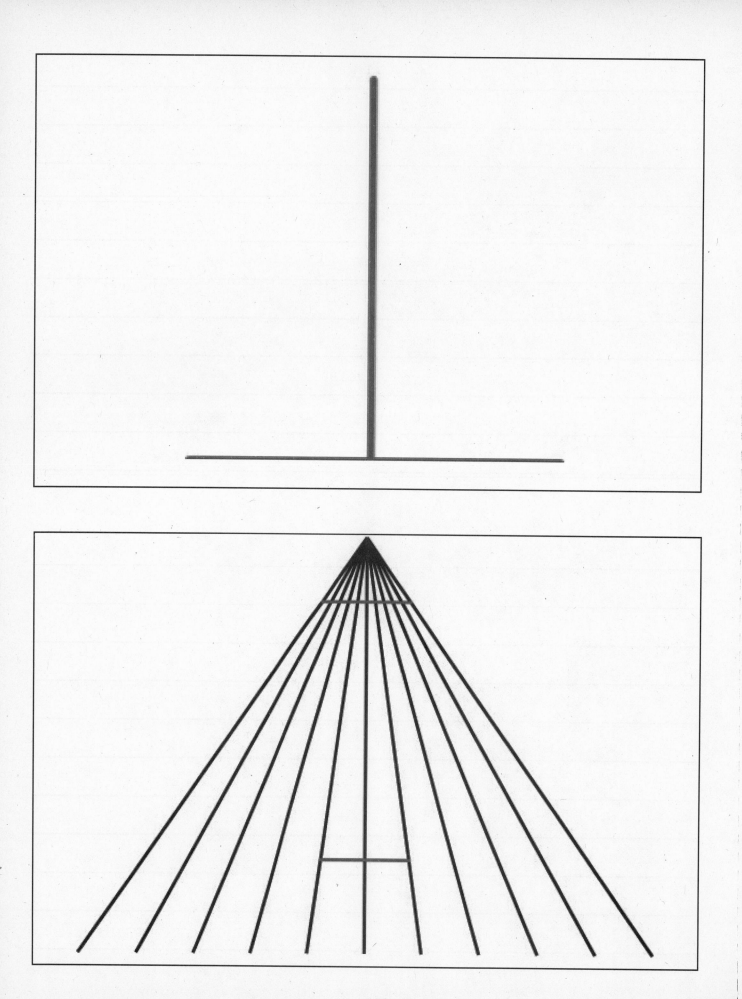

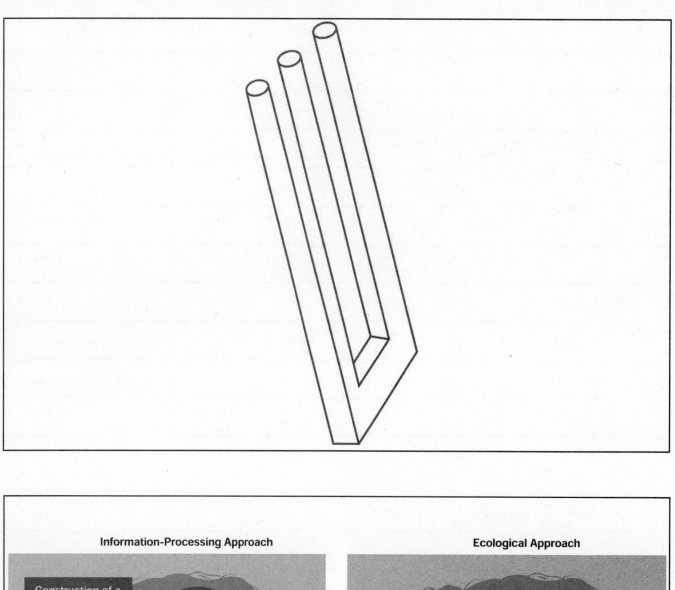

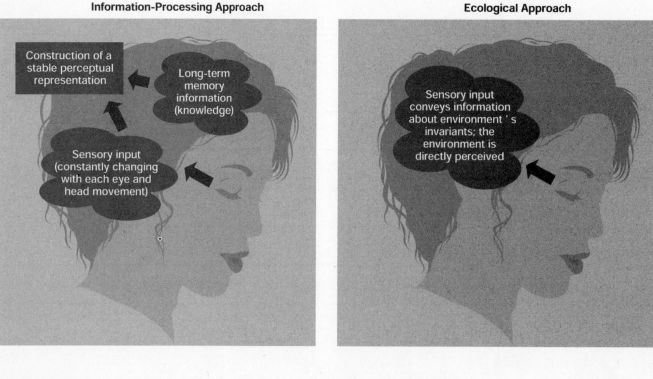

Information-Processing Approach

Construction of a stable perceptual representation

Long-term memory information (knowledge)

Sensory input (constantly changing with each eye and head movement)

Ecological Approach

Sensory input conveys information about environment's invariants; the environment is directly perceived

44

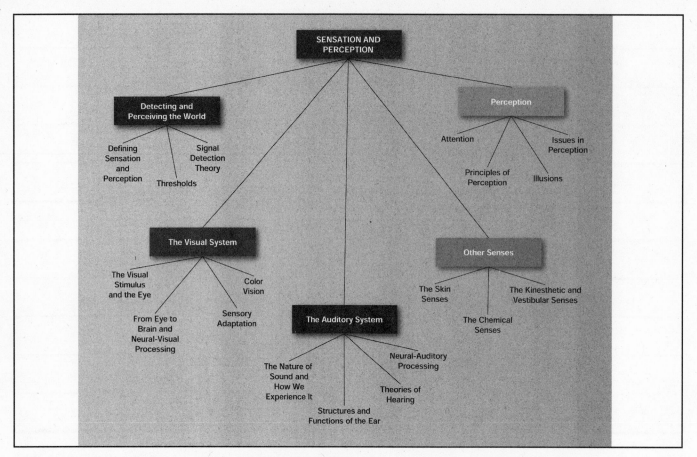

Chapter 5 States of Consciousness

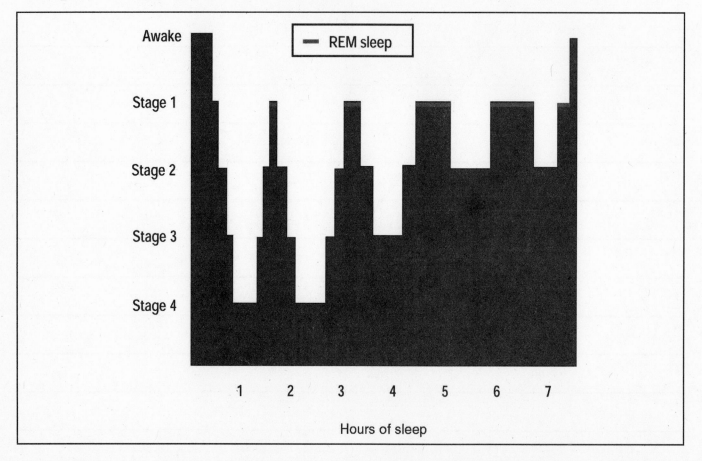

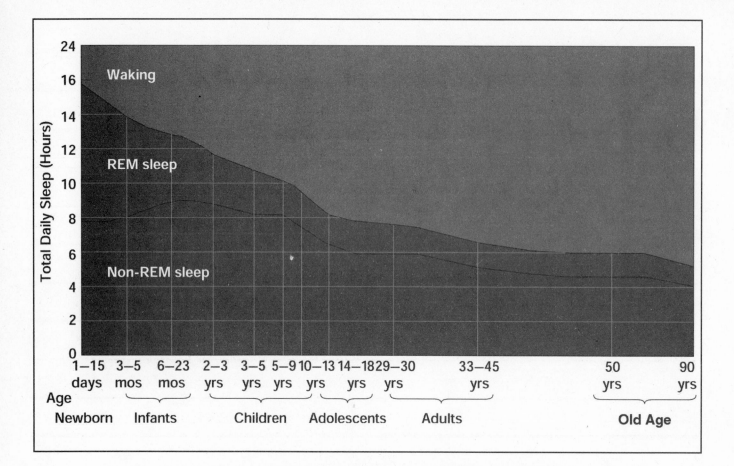

The sleep chart shows Total Daily Sleep (Hours) on the y-axis (0–24) with regions labeled "Waking," "REM sleep," and "Non-REM sleep," across age ranges on the x-axis:

Age: 1–15 days, 3–5 mos, 6–23 mos, 2–3 yrs, 3–5 yrs, 5–9 yrs, 10–13 yrs, 14–18 yrs, 29–30 yrs, 33–45 yrs, 50 yrs, 90 yrs

Categories: Newborn, Infants, Children, Adolescents, Adults, Old Age

One glass of wine equals one can of beer in alcoholic content.

Cocaine is extracted from coca plants.

Cannabis paraphernalia, drug equipment or gadgets, is usually sold in "head shops" for use in smoking marijuana.

Tranquilizers are used for reducing anxiety and inducing relaxation.

Amphetamines are stimulants used to increase alertness and energy.

Shown here is a private, illegal laboratory for manufacturing LSD.

DRUG CLASSIFICATION	MEDICAL USES	SHORT-TERM EFFECTS	OVERDOSE	HEALTH RISKS	RISK OF PHYSICAL/ PSYCHOLOGICAL DEPENDENCE
Depressants					
Alcohol	Pain relief	Relaxation, depressed brain activity, slowed behavior, reduced inhibitions	Disorientation, loss of consciousness, even death at high blood-alcohol levels	Accidents, brain damage, liver disease, heart disease, ulcers, birth defects	Physical: moderate; psychological: moderate
Barbiturates	Sleeping pill	Relaxation, sleep	Breathing difficulty, coma, possible death	Accidents, coma, possible death	Physical and psychological moderate to high
Tranquilizers	Anxiety reduction	Relaxation, slowed behavior	Breathing difficulty, coma, possible death	Accidents, coma, possible death	Physical: low to moderate; psychological: moderate to high
Opiates (narcotics)	Pain relief	Euphoric feelings, drowsiness, nausea	Convulsions, coma, possible death	Accidents, infectious diseases such as AIDS	Physical: high; psychological: moderate to high
Stimulants					
Amphetamines	Weight control	Increased alertness, excitability; decreased fatigue, irritability	Extreme irritability, feelings of persecution, convulsions	Insomnia, hypertension, malnutrition, possible death	Physical: possible; psychological: moderate to high
Cocaine	Local anesthetic	Increased alertness, excitability, euphoric feelings; decreased fatigue, irritability	Extreme irritability, feelings of persecution, convulsions, cardiac arrest, possible death	Insomnia, hypertension, malnutrition, possible death	Physical: possible; psychological: moderate (oral) to very high (injected or smoked)
Hallucinogens					
LSD	None	Strong hallucinations, distorted time perception	Severe mental disturbance, loss of contact with reality	Accidents	Physical: none; psychological: low
Marijuana	Treatment of the eye disorder glaucoma	Euphoric feelings, relaxation, mild hallucinations, time distortion, attention and memory impairment	Fatigue, disoriented behavior	Accidents, respiratory disease	Physical: very low; psychological: moderate

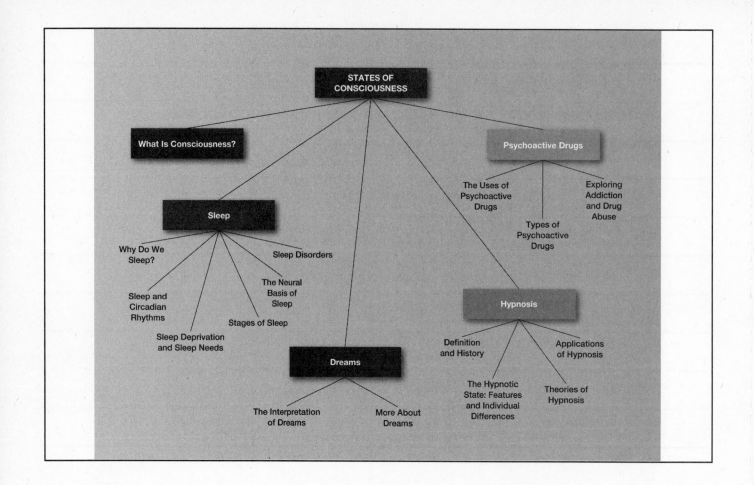

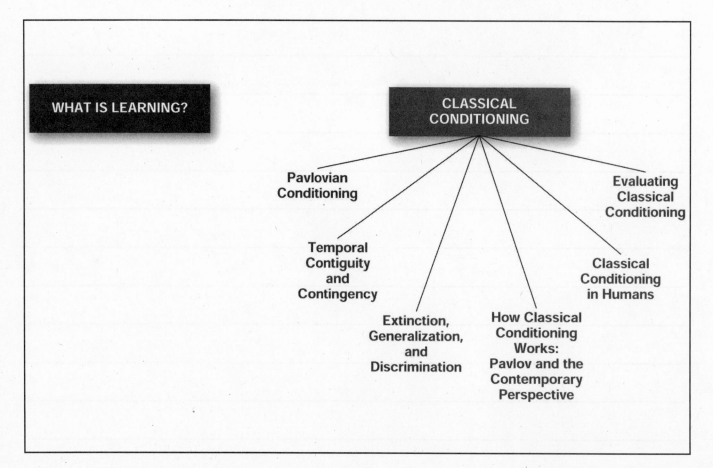

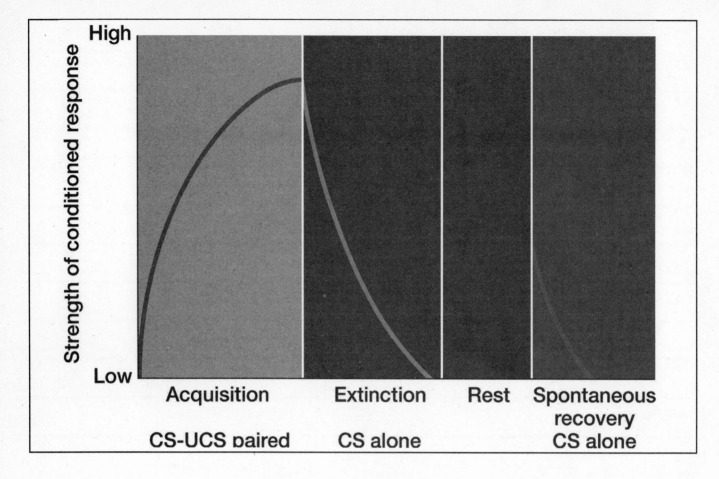

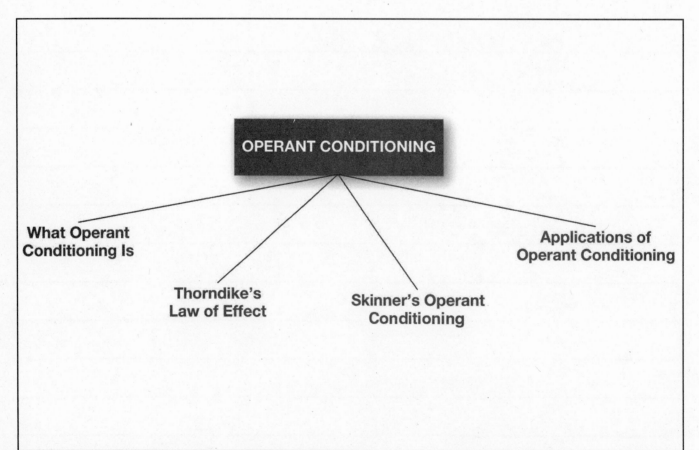

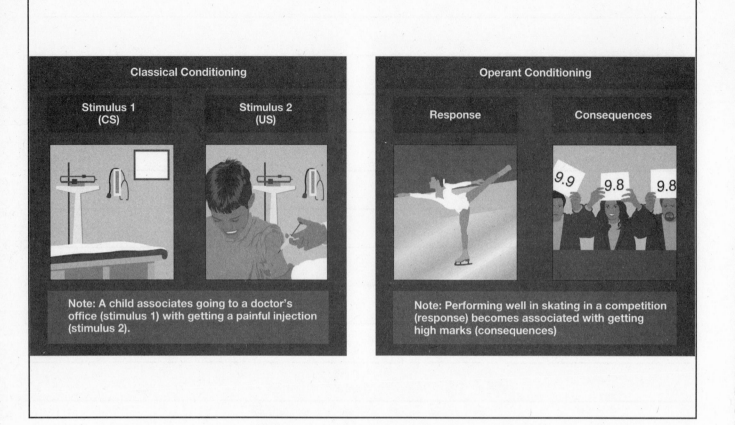

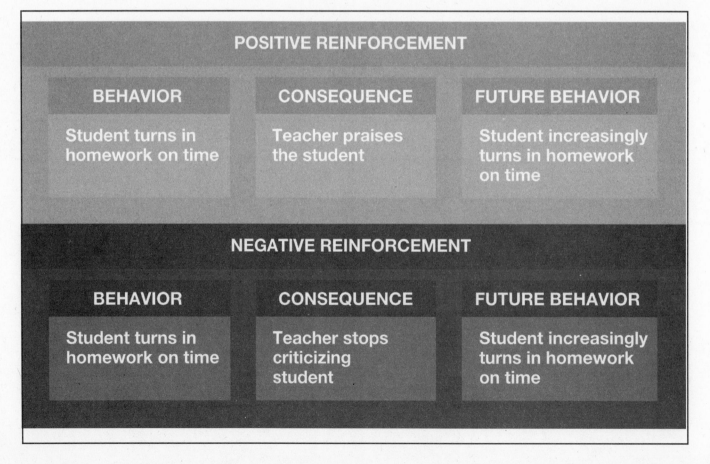

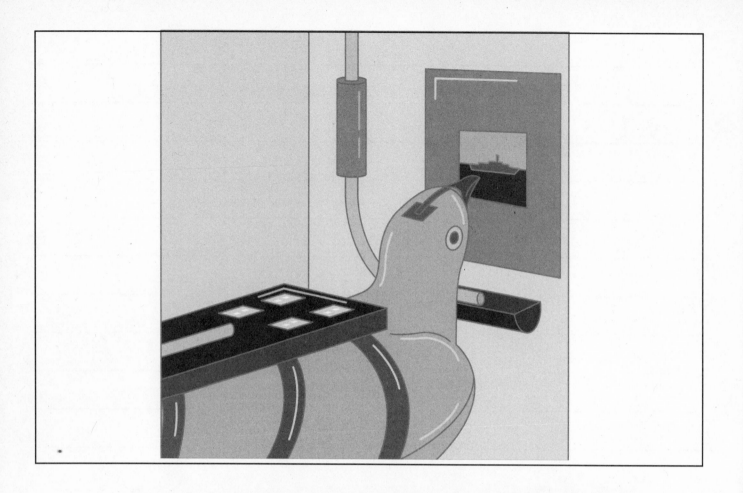

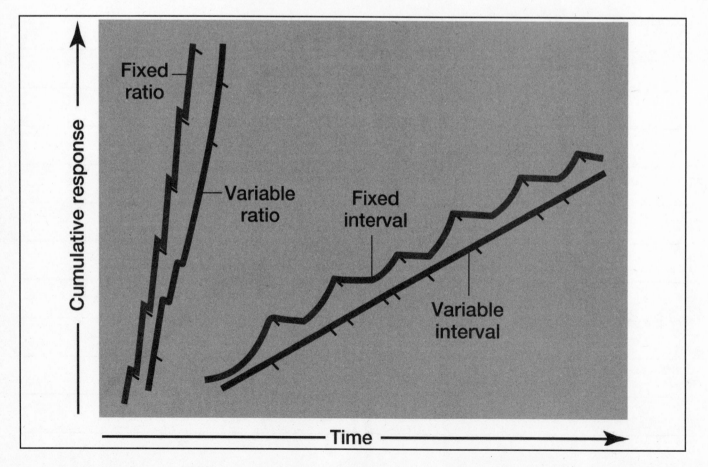

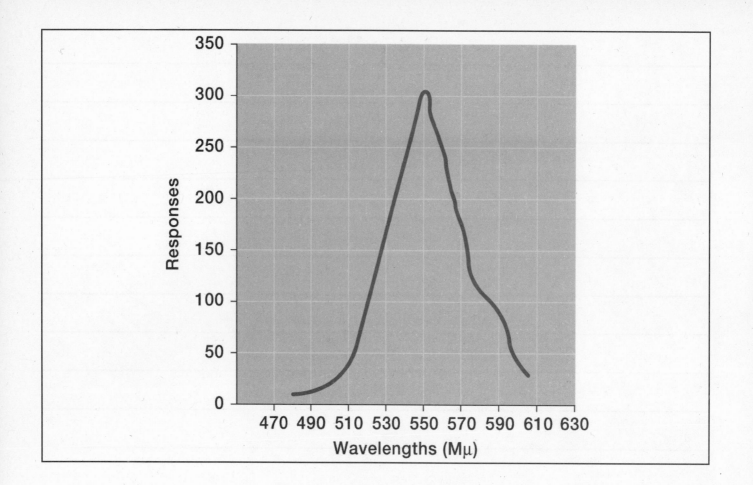

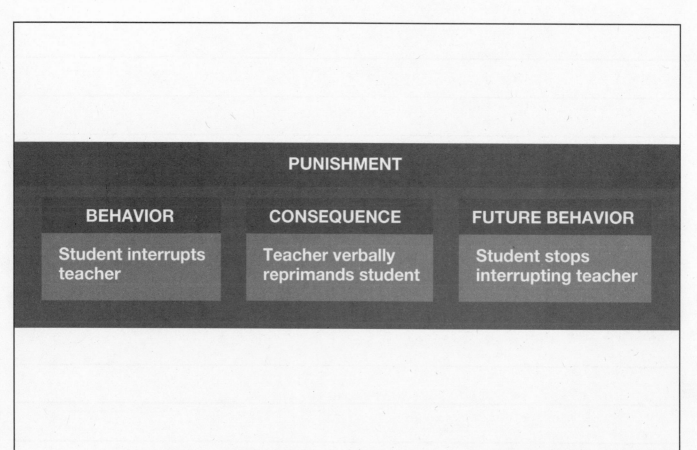

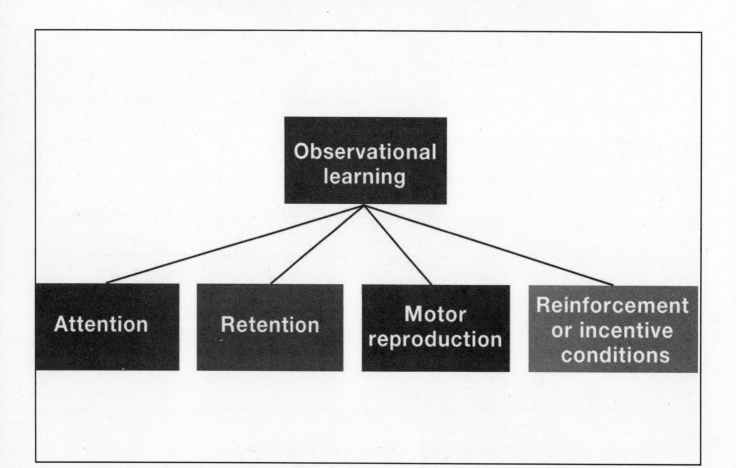

Stimulus

		PRESENTED	REMOVED
Behavior	INCREASES	Positive reinforcement (teacher praises student for turning in home-work on time)	Negative reinforcement (taking aspirin to get rid of pain)
	DECREASES	Positive punishment (spanking, criticizing)	Negative punishment (time-out, loss of privileges)

Observational learning

Attention

Retention

Motor reproduction

Reinforcement or incentive conditions

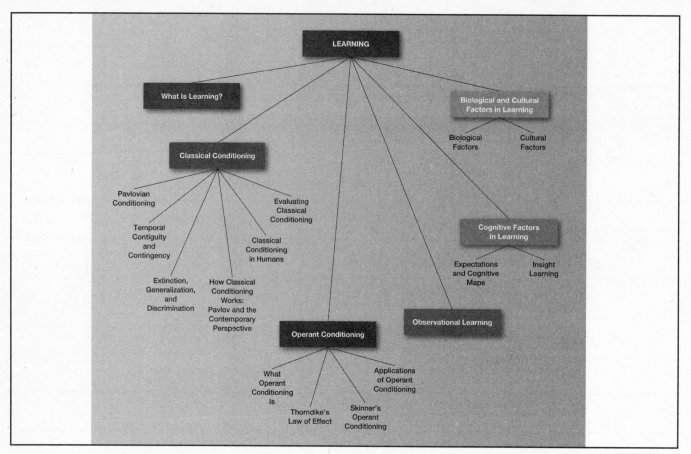

Chapter 7 Memory

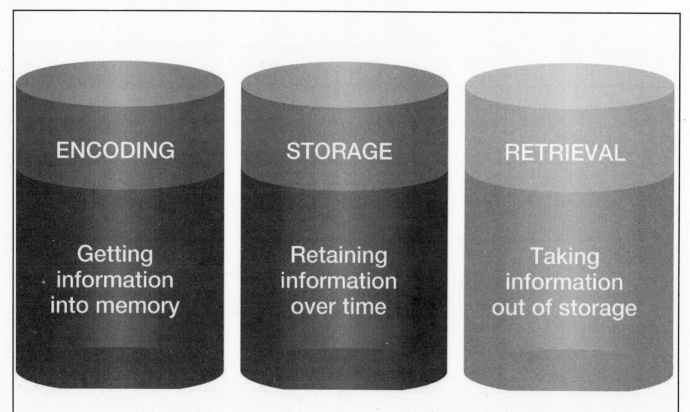

Depth of processing			
SHALLOW PROCESSING	Physical and perceptual features are analyzed.	The lines, angles, and contour that make up the physical appearance of an object, such as a car, are detected.	
INTERMEDIATE PROCESSING	Stimulus is recognized and labeled.	The object is recognized as a car.	
DEEP PROCESSING	Semantic, meaningful, symbolic characteristics are used.	Associations connected with car are brought to mind—you think about the Porsche or Ferrari you hope to buy or the fun you and friends had on spring break when you drove a car to the beach.	

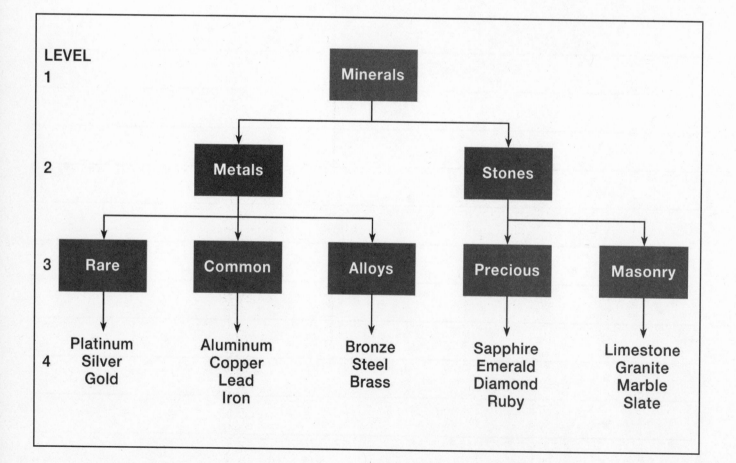

LEVEL 1 — Minerals

LEVEL 2 — Metals, Stones

LEVEL 3 — Rare, Common, Alloys, Precious, Masonry

LEVEL 4 —
Platinum Silver Gold
Aluminum Copper Lead Iron
Bronze Steel Brass
Sapphire Emerald Diamond Ruby
Limestone Granite Marble Slate

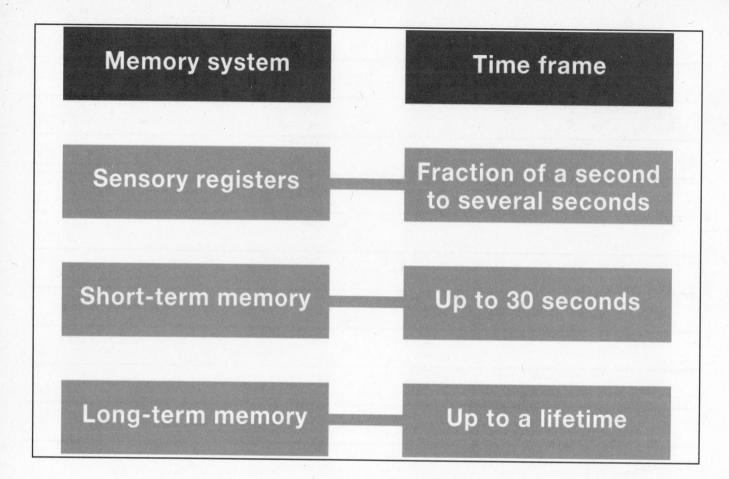

Memory system	Time frame
Sensory registers	Fraction of a second to several seconds
Short-term memory	Up to 30 seconds
Long-term memory	Up to a lifetime

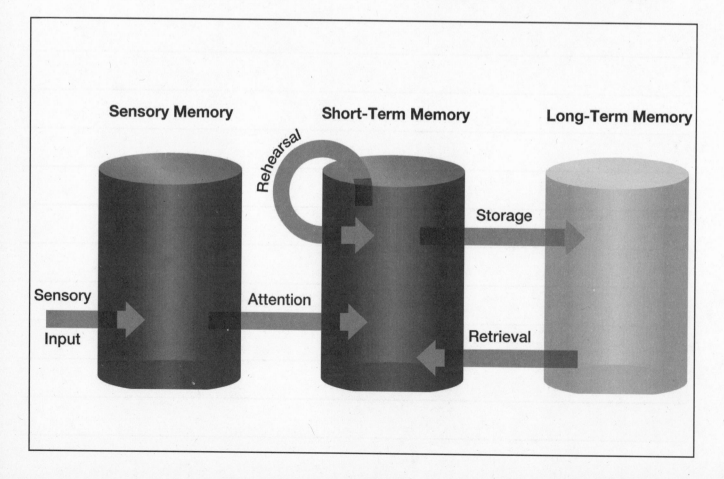

Sensory Memory

Short-Term Memory

Long-Term Memory

Rehearsal

Storage

Sensory

Input

Attention

Retrieval

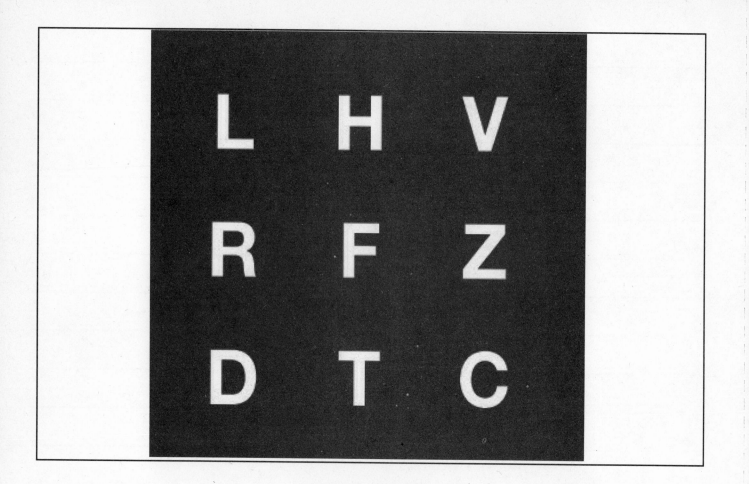

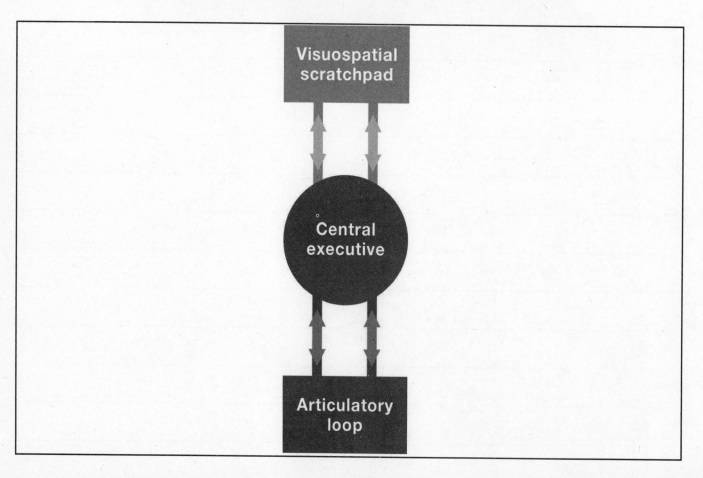

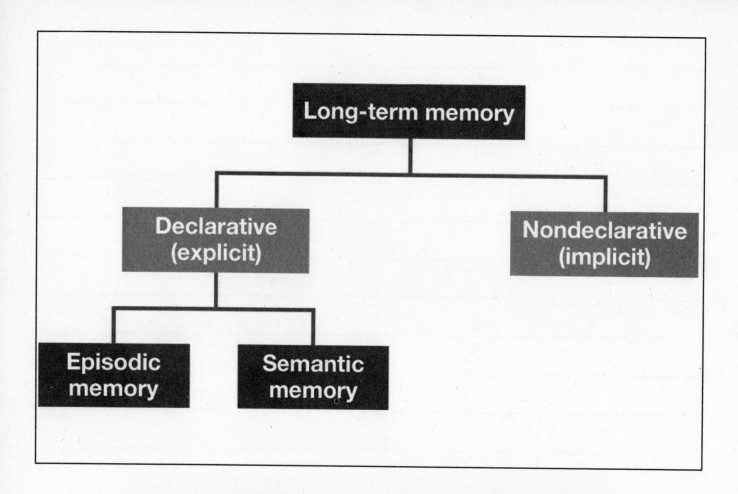

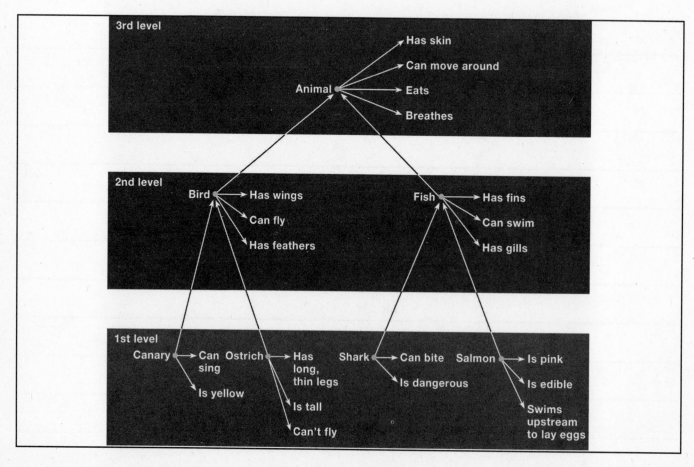

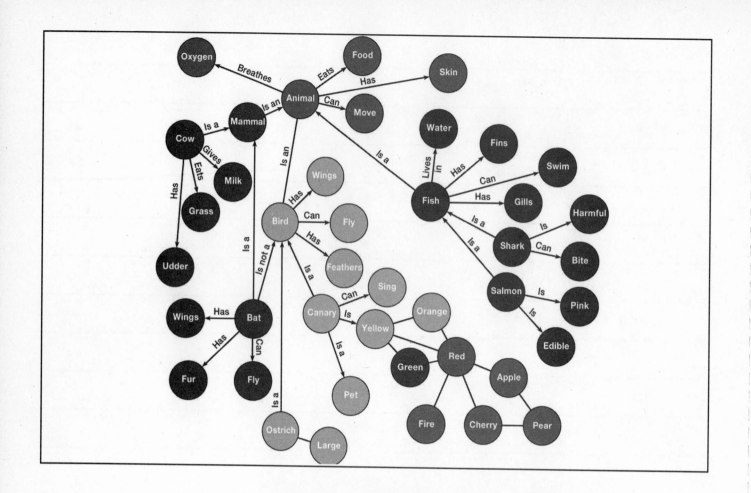

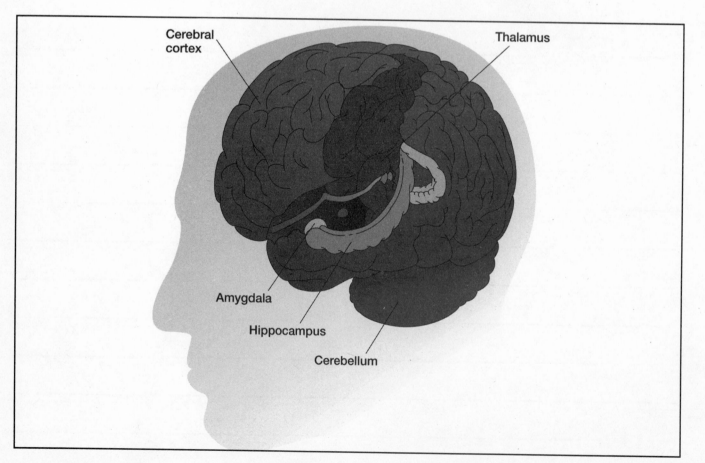

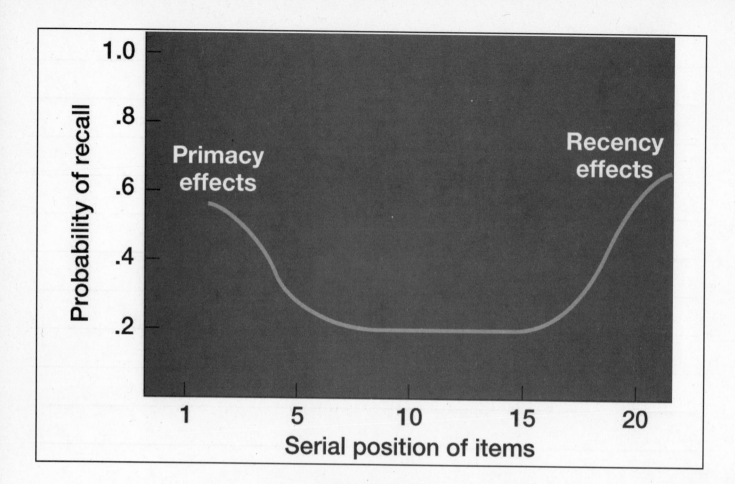

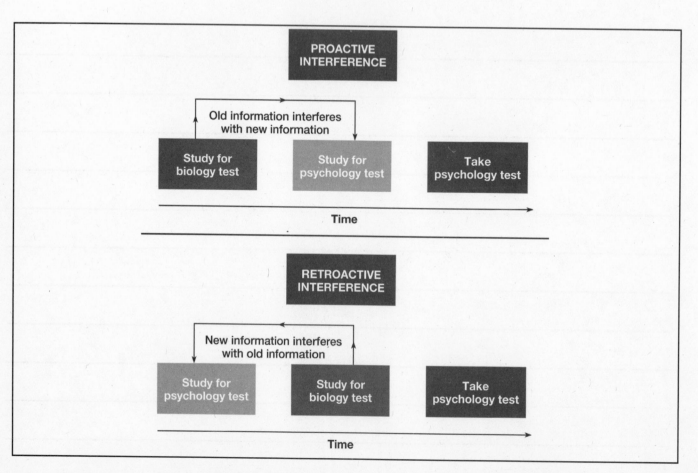

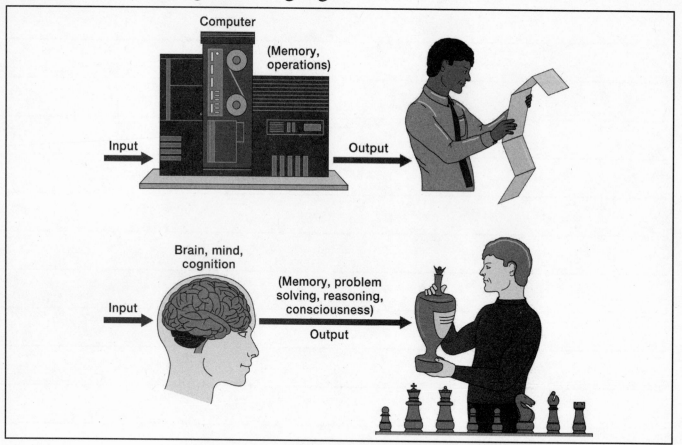

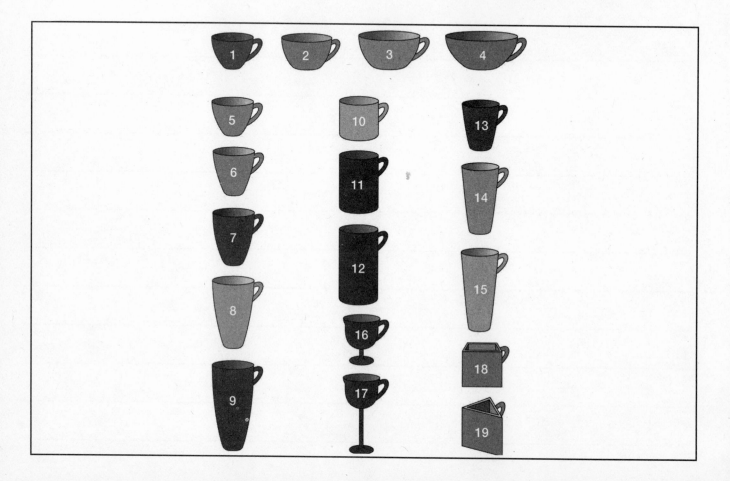

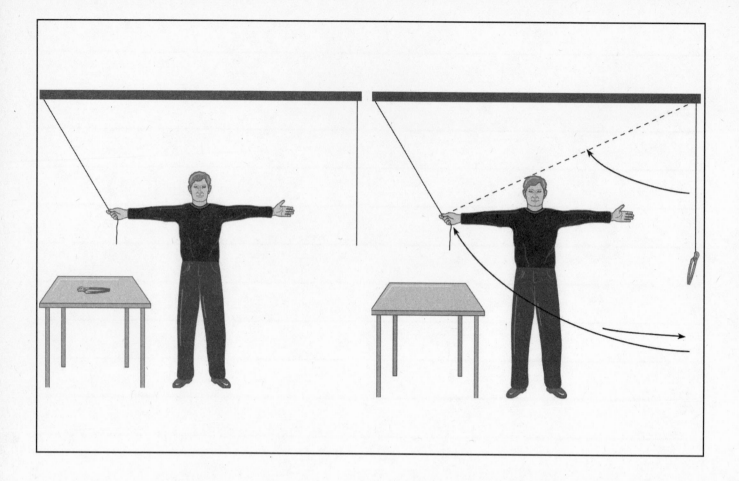

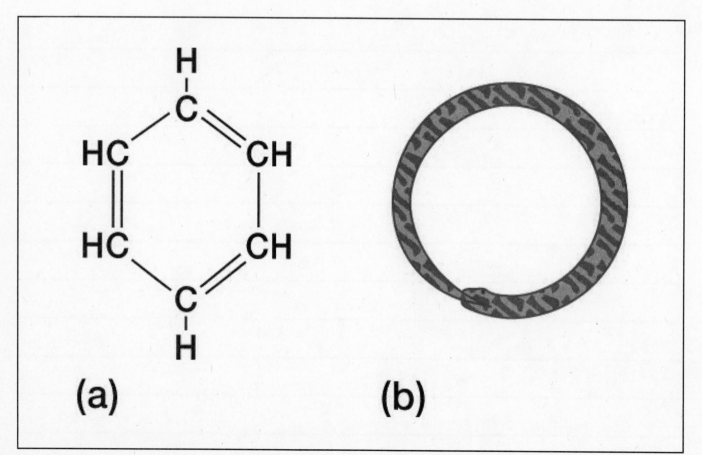

(a)

(b)

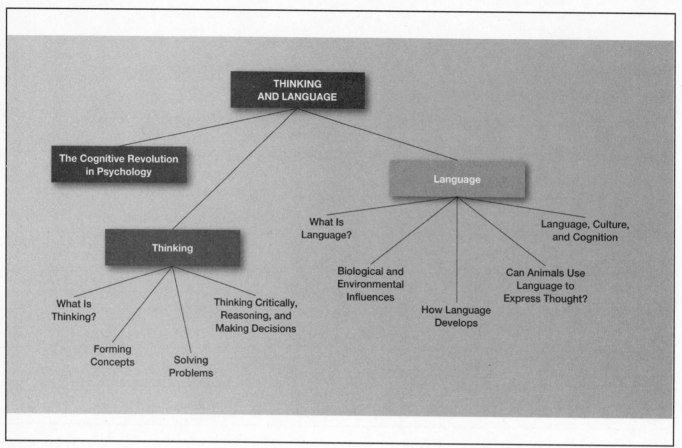

Chapter 9 Intelligence

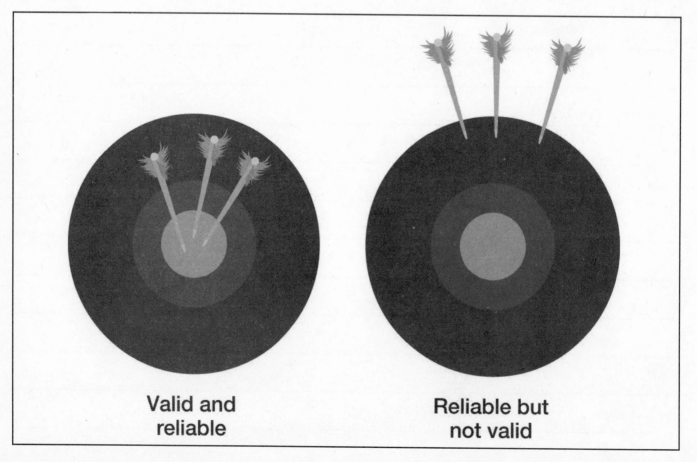

Valid and reliable

Reliable but not valid

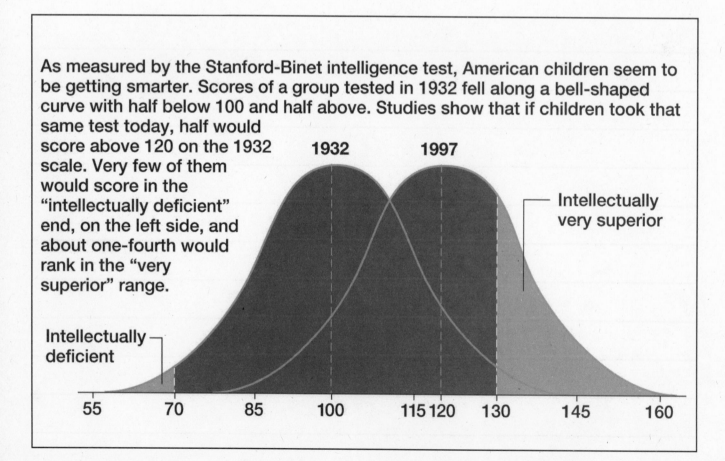

Percentage of cases under portions of the normal curve	0.13%	2.14%	13.59%	34.13%	34.13%	13.59%	2.14%	0.13%
Cumulative percentages	0.1%	2.3%	15.9%	50.0%	84.1%	97.7%	99.9%	
		2%	16%	50%	84%	98%		
Stanford-Binet IQs	52	68	84	100	116	132	148	

As measured by the Stanford-Binet intelligence test, American children seem to be getting smarter. Scores of a group tested in 1932 fell along a bell-shaped curve with half below 100 and half above. Studies show that if children took that same test today, half would score above 120 on the 1932 scale. Very few of them would score in the "intellectually deficient" end, on the left side, and about one-fourth would rank in the "very superior" range.

1932   1997

Intellectually very superior

Intellectually deficient

55   70   85   100   115 120   130   145   160

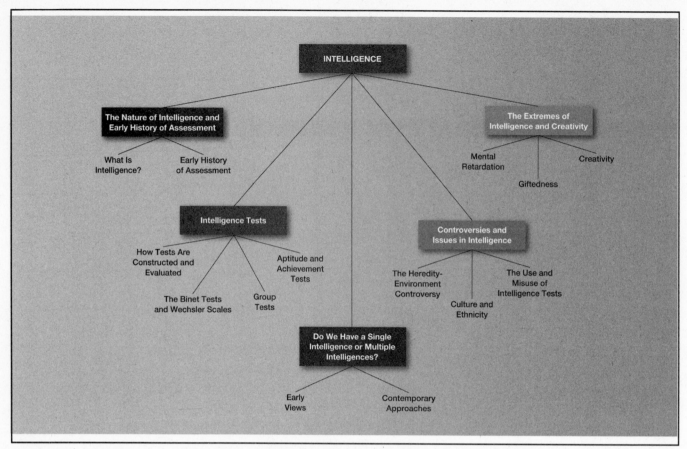

Chapter 10 Human Development

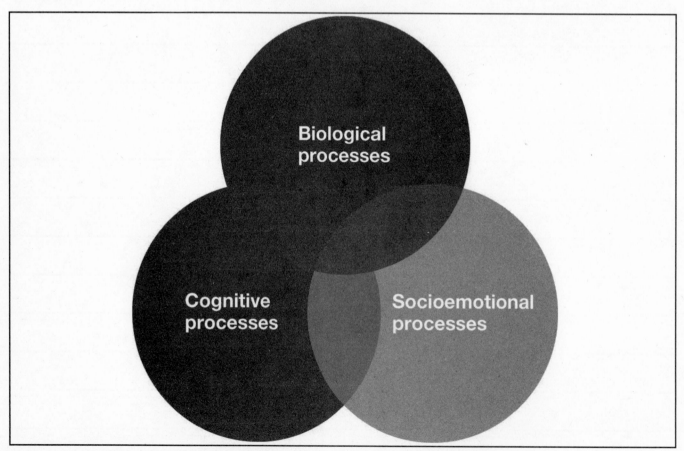

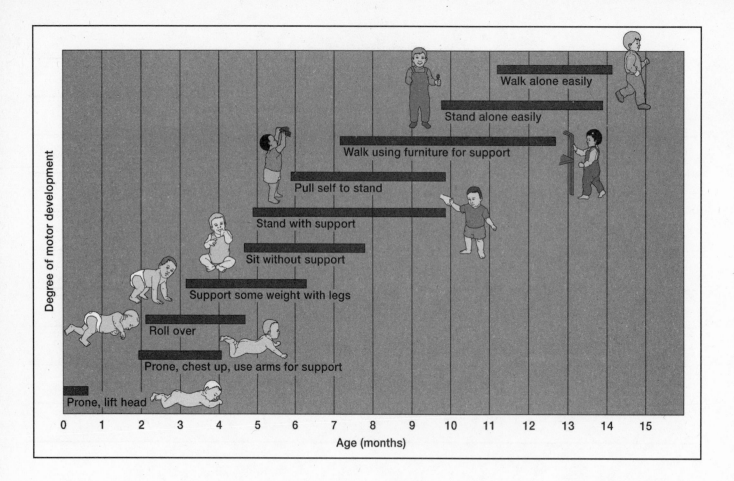

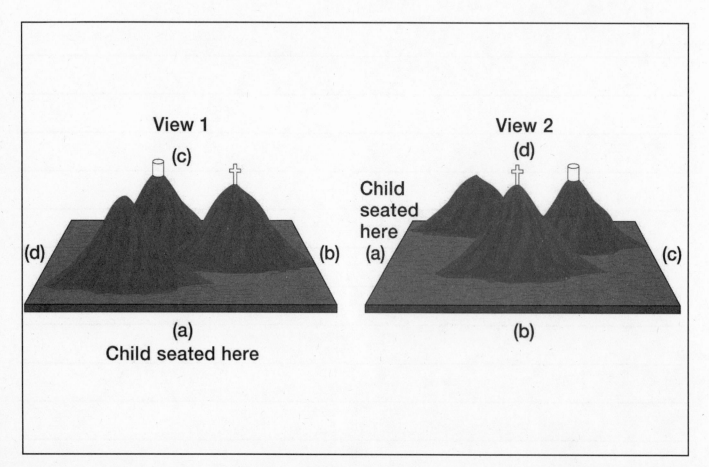

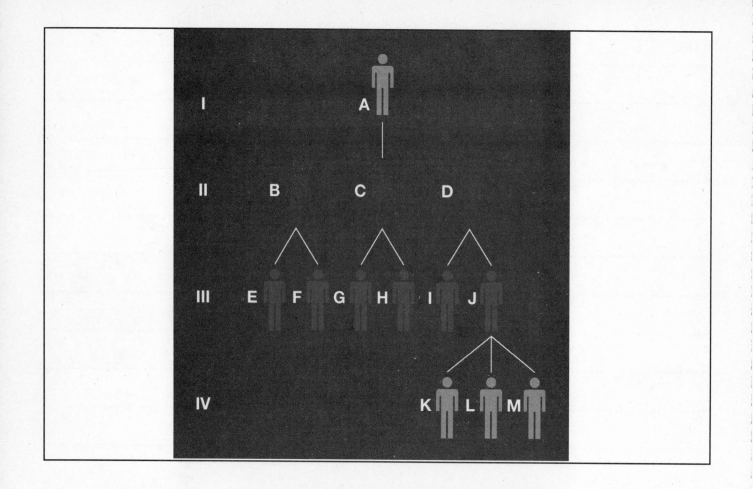

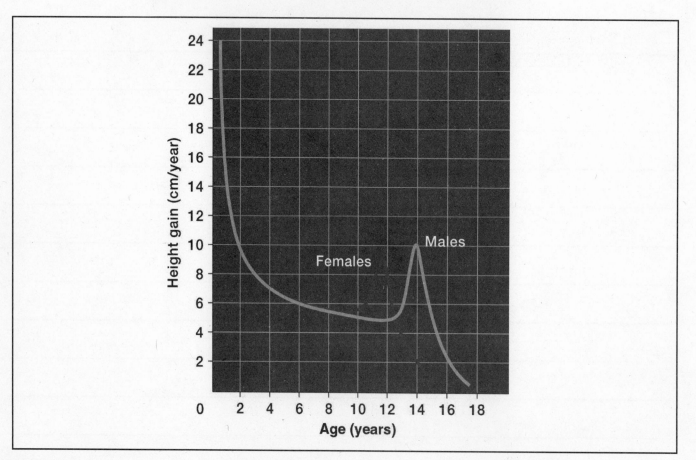

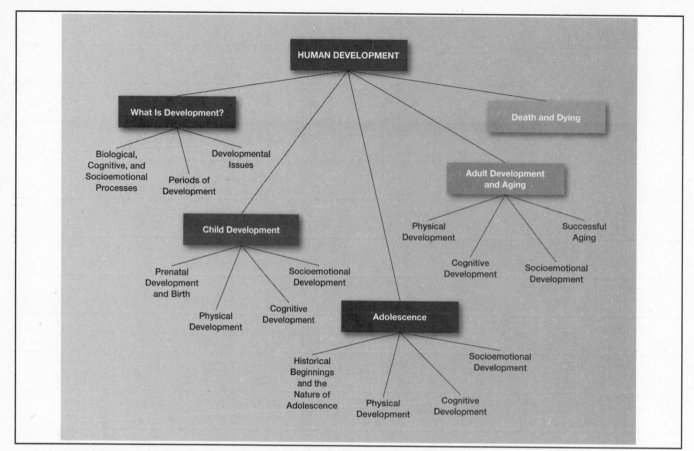

Chapter 11 Motivation and Emotion

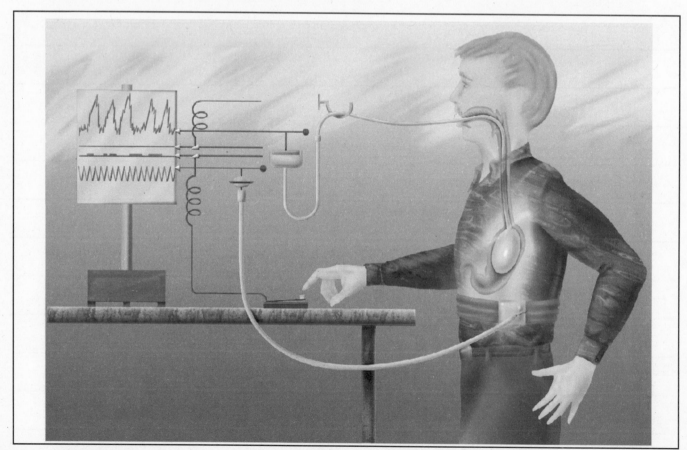

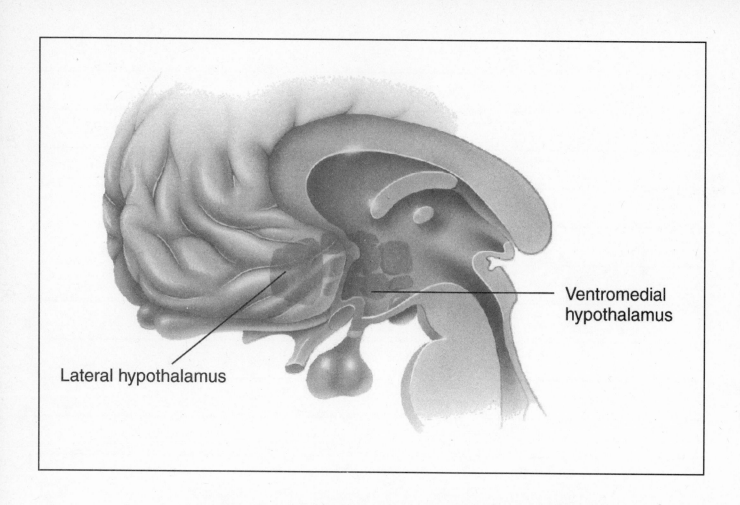

Ventromedial hypothalamus

Lateral hypothalamus

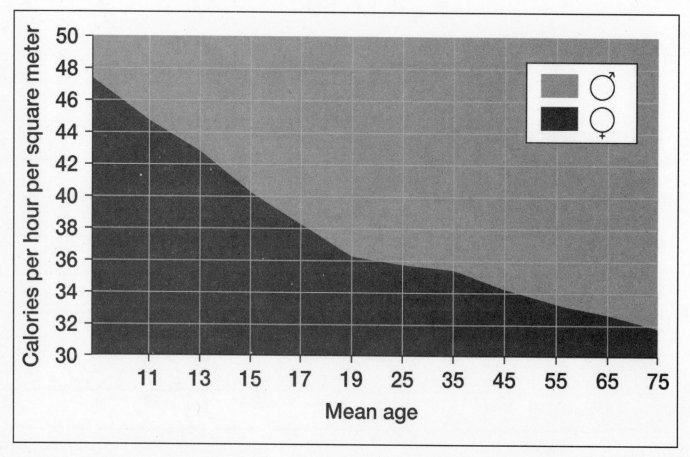

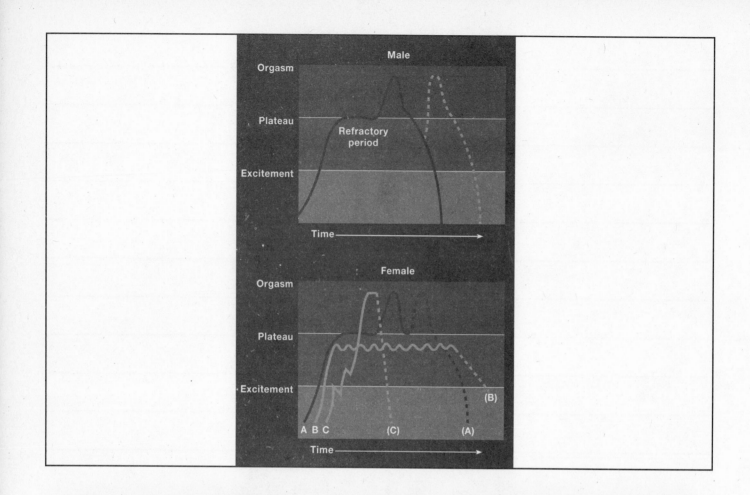

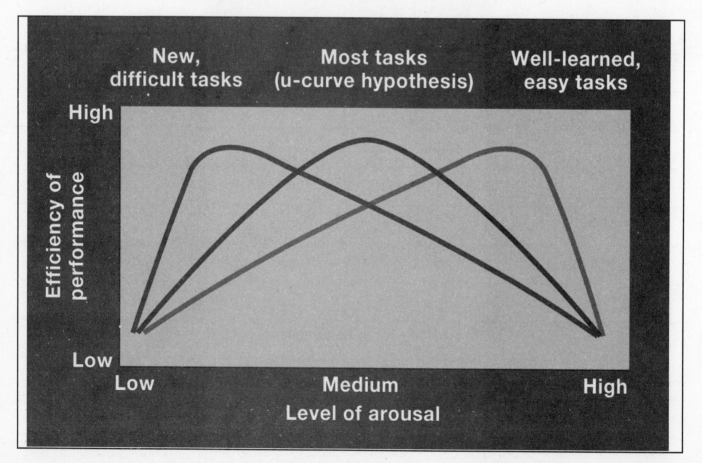

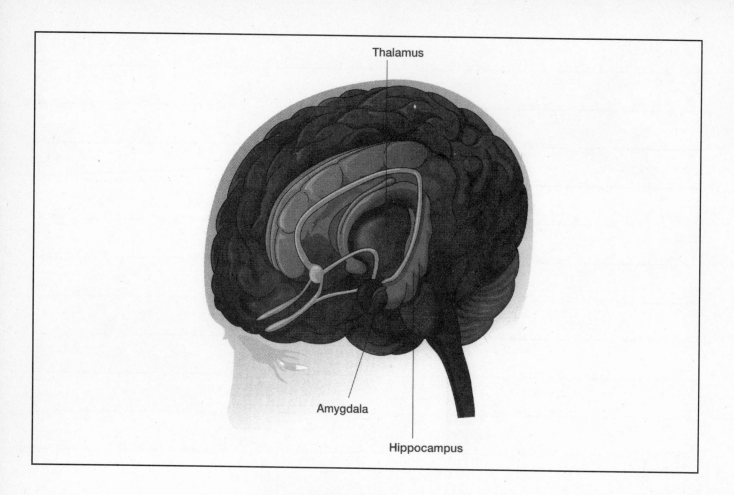

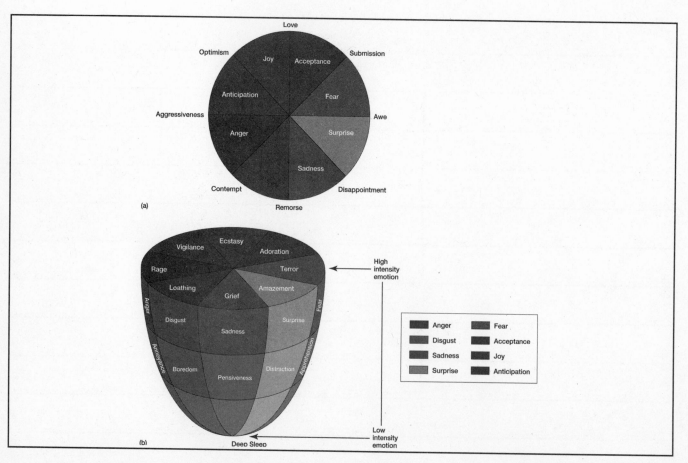

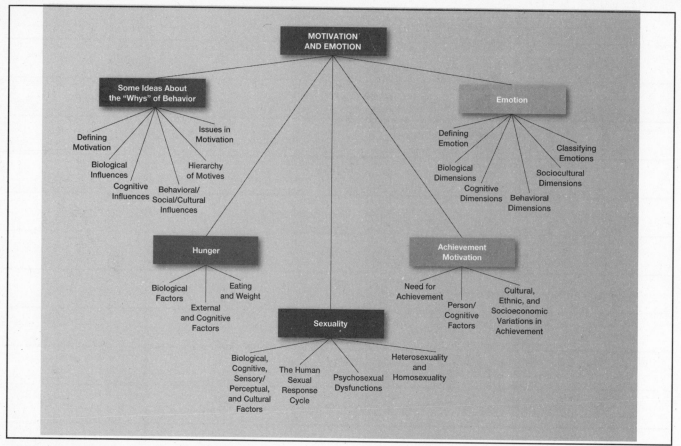

Chapter 12 Personality

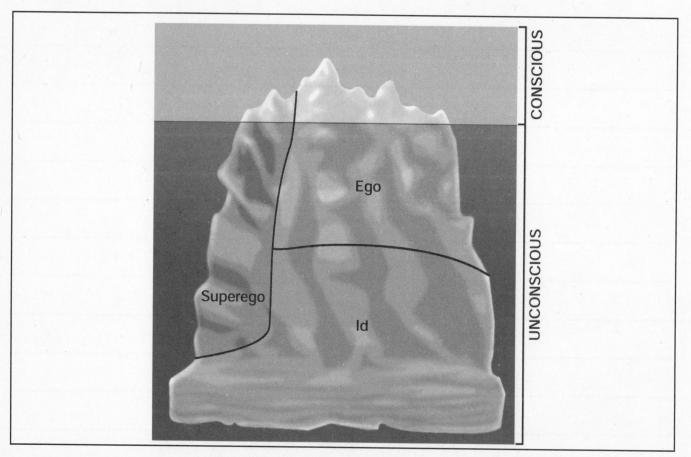

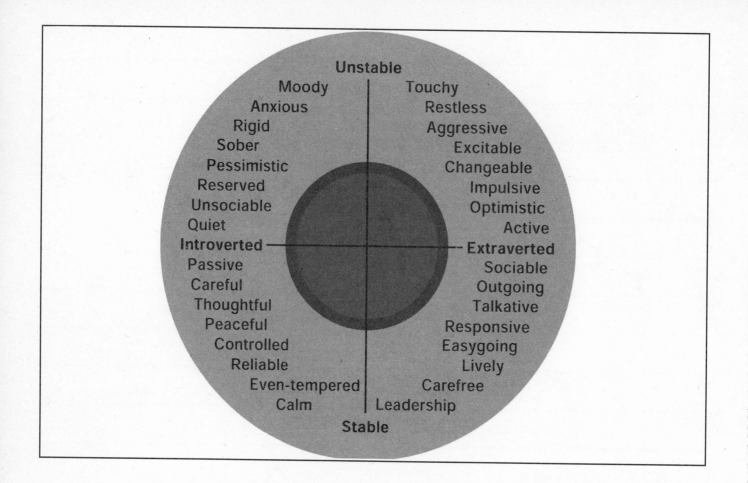

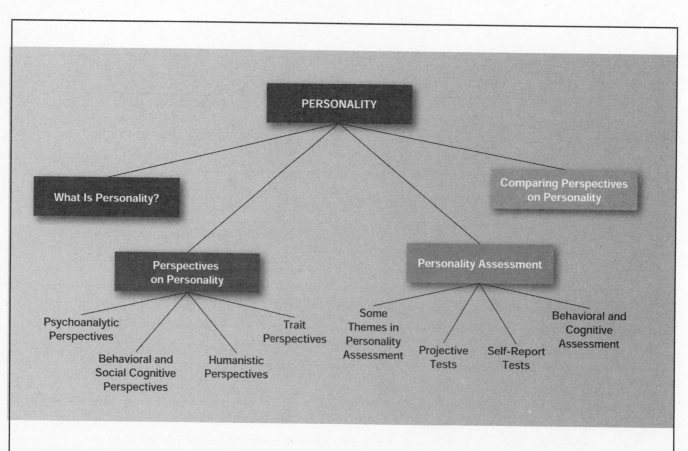

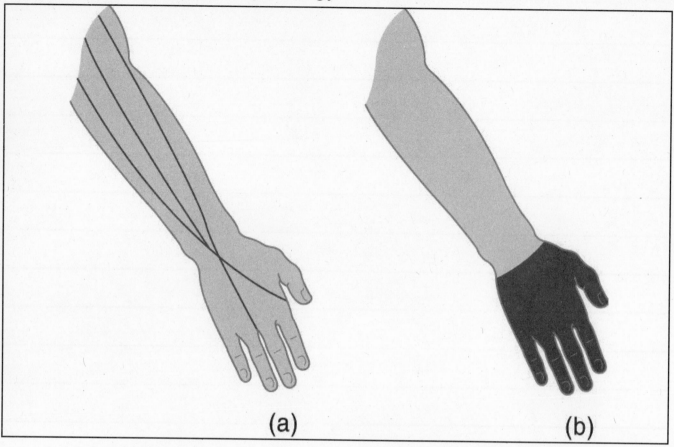

(a)   (b)

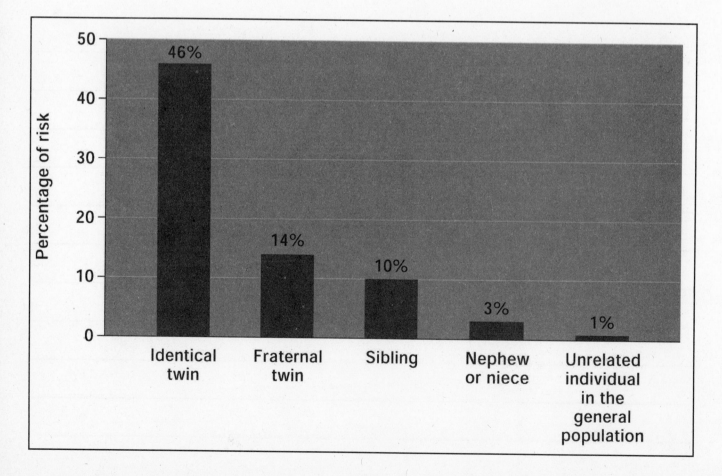

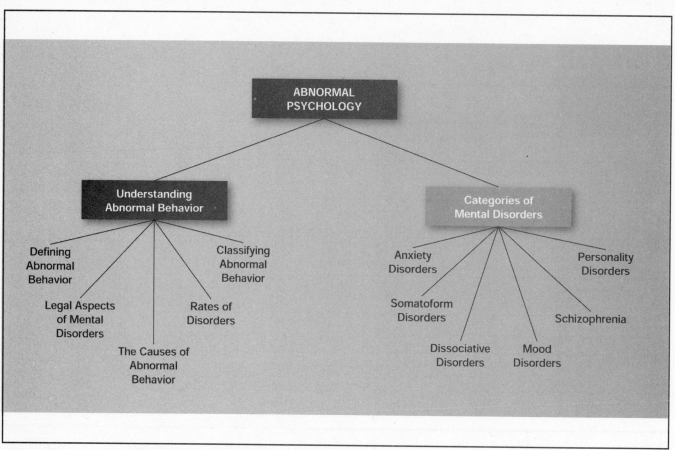

Chapter 14 Therapies

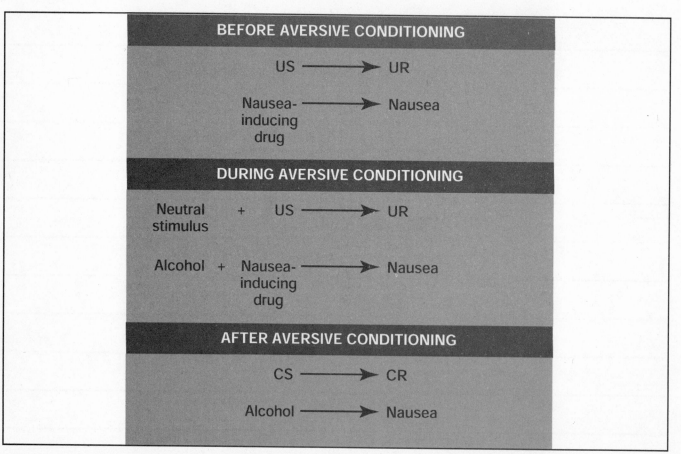

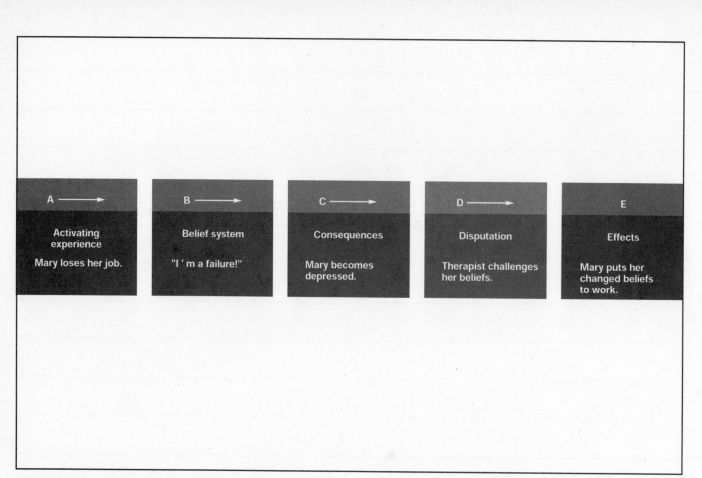

Chapter 15 Health Psychology

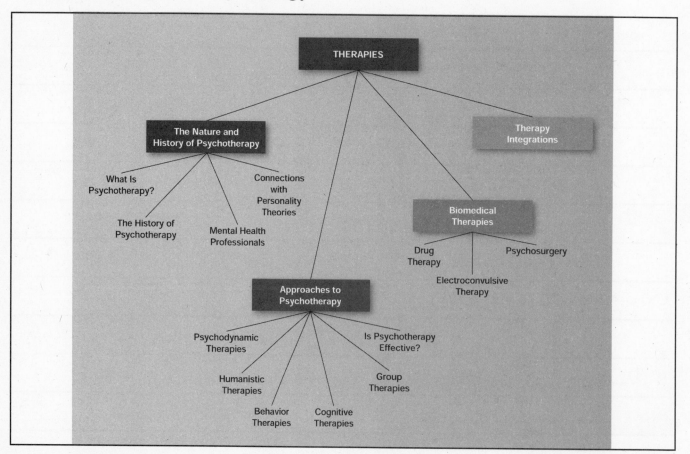

BIOLOGICAL FACTORS	PERSONALITY FACTORS	COGNITIVE FACTORS	ENVIRONMENTAL FACTORS	SOCIOCULTURAL FACTORS
Example: The body's response to stress	Example: How a person handles anger	Example: Whether a person perceives an event as threatening or challenging	Example: Frustrating stressors in the environment, such as being blocked from reaching a goal	Example: Living in poverty

Normal level of resistance to stress

1 Alarm stage

2 Resistance

3 Exhaustion

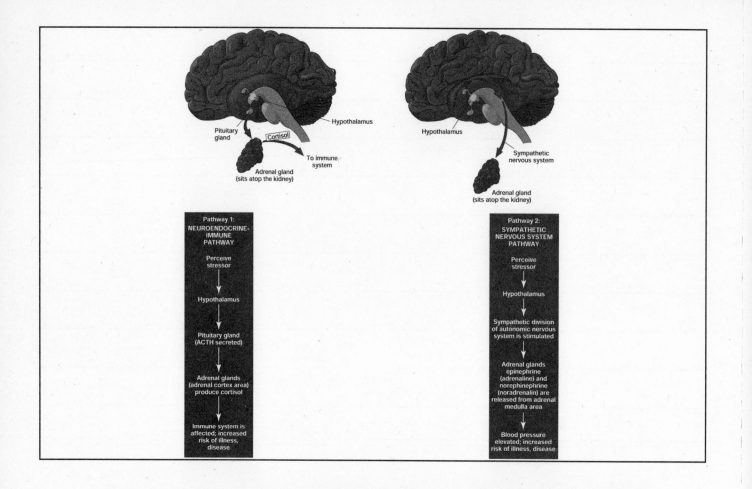

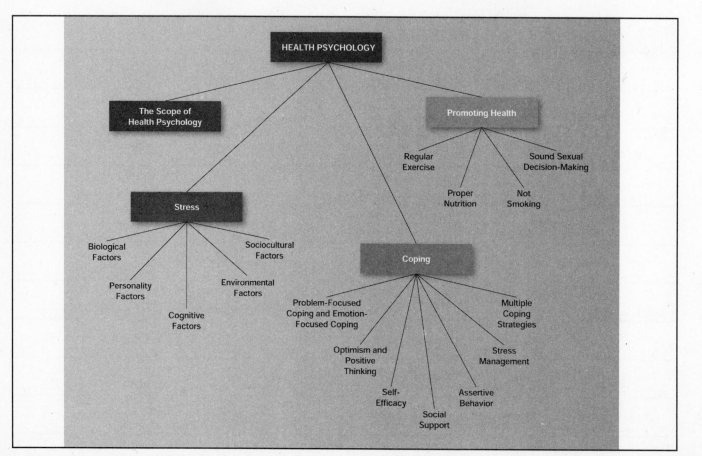

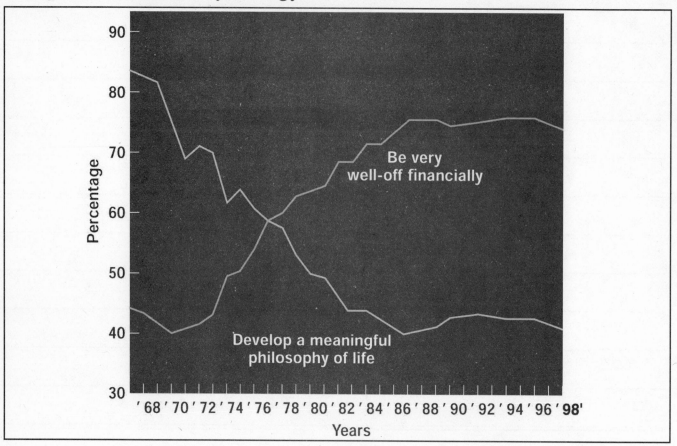

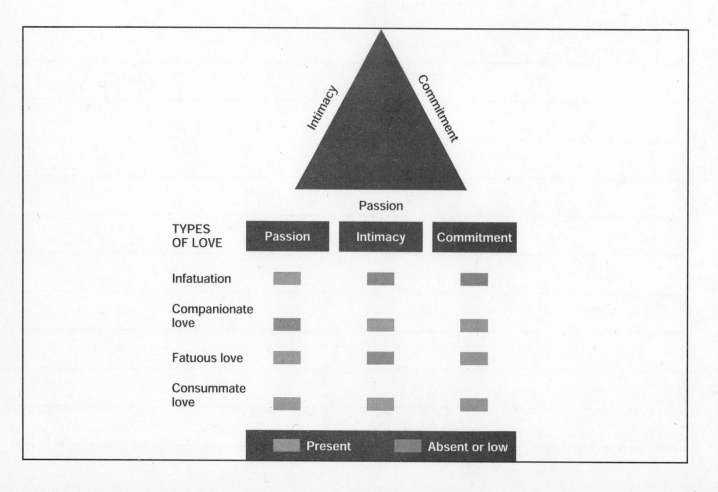

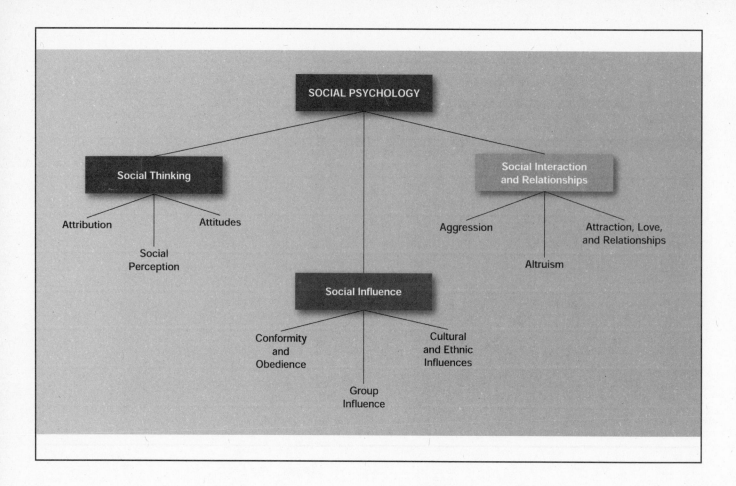